THE ORDER OF PRESENTATION IN PERSUASION

EDITED BY CARL I. HOVLAND

The Order of Presentation in Persuasion

BY

Carl I. Hovland

Wallace Mandell

Enid H. Campbell

Timothy Brock

Abraham S. Luchins

Arthur R. Cohen

William J. McGuire

Irving L. Janis

Rosalind L. Feierabend

Norman H. Anderson

New Haven and London, Yale University Press

Originally published
in Yale Studies in Attitude
and Communication.

PREFACE

FOR THE LAST TEN YEARS the writer and his colleagues have been engaged in a program of research seeking to improve our understanding of human psychological processes through the study of the effects which communication stimuli have upon attitudes and behavior. Our research on these problems began in a practical setting—in studying the effective utilization of training and indoctrinational films by the armed services during the war. Studies carried out under military auspices by Hovland, Lumsdaine, and Sheffield, were reported in 1949 under the title *Experiments on Mass Communication* (Princeton University Press). Opportunity for broader investigation of the influence process was afforded by a series of grants from the Rockefeller Foundation. Studies done under this program have been reported in a variety of technical journals. A progress report covering some of the highlights of the research program was presented by Hovland, Janis, and Kelley, in *Communication and Persuasion* (Yale University Press, 1953). Since then a sizable number of further investigations have been completed on a variety of interrelated topics. In the more recent studies an increasing emphasis is placed on evaluating the mediating processes involved in attitude change.

In considering plans for the publication of further studies it appeared to us wiser to have related researches reported together in monograph form rather than to have them scattered throughout a number of different technical journals.

Accordingly, a series of monographs has been planned which
will contain related research studies or new analyses of research problems. The present volume is the first of this pro-
jected series, and is devoted to an analysis of the effects upon
opinion and attitudes of different sequences of presentation
of communication materials. Subsequent volumes will deal
with personality factors in persuasibility, judgmental factors
underlying attitude change, and similar topics.

It is recognized that the type of publication involving con-
centration on a small delimited area represented in this
series is rather atypical in the field of social sciences, where
publications ordinarily treat topics of broad scope and generality. The present pattern is more commonly employed in
the natural sciences. The authors believe, however, that systematic exploration and variation on a single delimited topic
is particularly needed in the social sciences, where it often
takes a large number of related studies on a single issue to
define the major variables and to test some of their important
interrelationships. Repetition with strategic variation is also
needed to test the generality of propositions suggested by a
single study. Only through the development of small well-
analyzed systems will larger, more comprehensive, future
systematizations be possible. By concentrating a series of coordinated studies on a limited set of problems, such as that
of primacy vs. recency in persuasion, it becomes possible to
explore the values and limitations of a variety of theoretical
approaches and to obtain the necessary empirical anchorage
for developing fruitful theoretical innovations.

The authors are indebted to a large number of individuals and groups. First of all we are grateful to the Rockefeller
Foundation for generous support of our work, which has
enabled us to develop a long-range program rather than hav-

ing to conform to the frequent pattern of financing separately single small-scale projects. Their grant enables us not only to carry out the program of studies here at Yale but to support studies by investigators elsewhere who wish to carry out researches that can be coordinated with our own. Thus the studies reported in the present volume by Abraham Luchins of the University of Oregon were supported by funds supplied through our grant. The advantages of this type of cooperative research appear to us very substantial.

We are also indebted to Mark A. May, Director of the Institute of Human Relations, for facilities for prosecuting our studies and for support of the present volume. The cooperation of teachers and principals of the large number of schools in which the studies were carried out is gratefully acknowledged; without their support research of this type could not be effectively prosecuted. Rosalind L. Feierabend helped greatly in improving the style and readability of many of the chapters, David Horne of the Yale Press was responsible for the preparation of the manuscript for publication, and Leonard Doob contributed substantially as a general reader-critic. Fred Sheffield and Robert Abelson also deserve our thanks for careful reading of the manuscript and for numerous helpful suggestions. Finally our gratitude is expressed to Marcia Ennis and Sally Wilson for the typing of the entire manuscript and to Jane Olejarczyk for assistance at the inevitable critical phases of preparation.

CARL I. HOVLAND

March 15, 1957

CONTENTS

ix

CHAPTER 1

Introduction

CARL I. HOVLAND

MANY FACTORS INFLUENCE the effectiveness of a communication: the reputation of the communicator and of the medium which he employs, the receptivity and predispositions of the audience, the actual content of the message, and, importantly, matters of organization and procedure.

This book is concerned with one of the major organizational, procedural factors: the effect which order of presentation has upon an audience. When the problem is stated in this general form, it is clear that "order" can refer to two different kinds of variation: (1) the order of presenting a series of communications and (2) the order of presenting the various elements within a single communication. The investigations here reported include phases of both variations.

An example of the first is one where a controversial issue is being discussed in which the advocates of both sides seek to present their views as forcefully as possible. An important question for research here is to determine the circumstances under which it is advantageous to present a communication before the opposition has an opportunity to reach the audience or afterward, in order to have "the last say." Involved is the relative impact on opinion of "primacy" and "recency."

The second type may be illustrated by situations in which one side of an issue is being advocated by a single communicator. Here he seeks the optimal organization of his material. He must decide, for example, whether he should begin with those arguments which favor his side of the issue and subsequently refute opposing arguments *or* whether he should dispose of the opposition before offering his own positive arguments.

At present scientific principles in the field of communication are not sufficiently developed to provide clear-cut answers to such problems and further research is required. As the authors stated in *Communication and Persuasion* (18):

> Answering questions of this sort at present is much more of an art than a science, but the underlying factors upon which the effects of alternative ways of organizating a message depend are ones which are of considerable concern to the scientist interested in communication.
>
> The theoretical factors underlying the choice of alternative organizations do not constitute a closely integrated system, but require reference to a large number of principles of attention, perception, motivation, and learning. . . . [These problems] are theoretically complex and only a small beginning has been made in unraveling the numerous factors involved. [p. 99]

The present series of studies is devoted to the task of helping to unravel some of these complexities.

Order Effects in Presentation of Successive Communications

Interest in the problem of order of presentation in the type of communication situation where both sides of a controversial issue are presented goes back to the publication in 1925 of a study by Lund (34). On the basis of his research he enunciated a Law of Primacy in Persuasion, stating that the side of an issue presented first will have greater effectiveness than the side presented subsequently. He had given his classes of college students a mimeographed communication in support of one side of a controversial issue (e.g. "a protective tariff is a wise policy for the United States") and had then presented a second communication advocating a diametrically opposed stand on the same issue. He discovered that the communication coming first (whether pro or con) influenced the students significantly more than the one coming second.

Subsequent experiments, however, have not always obtained this outcome. Cromwell (7), for example, performed a study in which affirmative and negative speeches on socialized medicine and labor arbitration were presented to groups of students whose opinions were measured before and after the talks. A significantly greater change was produced in the direction of that side of the issue presented last. Thus this investigator obtained a "recency effect" rather than a "primacy effect."

The difference in the outcome of these two experiments and the pronounced variability in results obtained in a replication of the Lund experiment by Hovland and Mandell have led the present authors to the conclusion that it is premature at present to postulate a Law of Primacy.[1] Rather

1. Lund's factor of "primacy in persuasion" should be distinguished from "primacy" in serial learning, in which early parts of a serial learning task are better remembered than the middle of the series (cf. 16, pp. 623–4). The tendency for the first items to be remembered best was thought to be a manifestation of a general "law of primacy." The last items in a list are also better remembered than those in the middle. This was then ascribed to a "law of recency": cf. Carr (5). Lund's analysis involves only two communications, one pro and one con. So if either the first or the second is superior, we

they believe an attempt should be made to determine the conditions which operate to make the first side more effective under some circumstances, the second under others, and both sides equally effective under still others. Accordingly a series of experiments was conducted to assess the influence of certain variables on the relative prevalence of primacy or recency effects in persuasive communications. These studies are reported in Part I (Chapters 2, 3, 4 and 5).

The general problem raised in the experiments reported in Part I is the influence of various activities and instructions which are introduced before the presentation of alternative sides of an issue or during the interval between the two communications. In the research described in Chapter 2 the effect of inserting an anonymous questionnaire between the pro and con communications was investigated. Expressing one's opinion on a questionnaire after only a single side has been heard might "commit" the recipient to the position he adopts after the first communication. Since the Lund and the Cromwell studies differed with respect to whether they did or did not incorporate an intervening questionnaire, it was hoped that this study would help to explain the different outcomes in the two experiments. A more intense type of commitment to a position after hearing only one side of an issue was also investigated. Primacy effects were investigated among (a) experimental subjects who were asked to write out their opinions for subsequent publication in a magazine read by their peers, and (b) control subjects who wrote their opinions under conditions of anonymity (Chapter 3).

The activities introduced in the preceding experiments would be expected to *increase* the extent of primacy effect. Activities and instructions which would be expected to *de-*

---

are bound to have either primacy or recency: the question is, which of the two has the greater impact on opinion.

crease the amount of primacy effect were also studied, and these experiments are reported in Chapters 4 and 5. Contradictory communications about the personality and behavior of an individual unknown to the subject were presented successively with and without prior warning as to potential conflict in the material. Warning as to the fallibility of "first impressions" was given to one group before either communication and to another group between the two conflicting blocks of information.

Order Effects within a Communication

The second general class of problems is that concerned with the order of presentation within a single communication. These investigations are reported in Part II (Chapters 6, 7, and 8). There are also, of course, a very large number of possible variables in this situation. Only three are chosen for investigation here:

(1) When a presentation on one side of an issue involves both arousal of "drive" and giving of information concerning the issue, what is the effect upon opinion change of drive arousal followed by information as compared with presentation of information followed by drive arousal? A study of this problem is reported in Chapter 6. The author also analyzes the relationship between the order of presentation of these elements and the motivational pattern of his subjects.

(2) When the same communicator transmits a series of messages involving several different attitudes, some of which the audience finds highly desirable and others undesirable, what are the effects of introducing the desirable first and then the undesirable as compared with the reverse order? Experimental data bearing on this problem are discussed in Chapter 7.

(3) When a communicator who is highly respected by his

audience wishes to include both pro and con arguments on the same issue, what is the effect of introducing the pro arguments first as compared with that of introducing first con arguments which are not initially salient for the audience? An investigation of this topic is presented in Chapter 8. The theory underlying this research is elaborated in Appendix B.

Practical Implications

The problem of order of presentation in communication is of more than academic interest. Should primacy obtain to any significant extent, there would be important practical implications for a variety of situations. Doob, for example, postulates the operation of primacy in propaganda:

> The propagandist scores an initial advantage whenever his propaganda reaches people before that of his rivals. . . . readers or listeners are then biased to comprehend, forever after, the event as it has been initially portrayed to them. If they are told in a headline or a flash that the battle has been won, the criminal has been caught, or the bill is certain to pass the legislature, they will usually expect subsequent information to substantiate this first impression. When later facts prove otherwise, they may be loath to abandon what they believe to be true until, perhaps, the evidence becomes overwhelming [10, pp. 421–2].

Another propaganda device which assumes primacy is that used by politicians in "smearing" an opponent. Their expectation is that even if the evidence subsequently refutes the allegation, the initial charge will still have inflicted considerable damage. Political beliefs have been attributed in part to primacy effects:

Whether we are democrats or republicans, Protestants or Catholics, is frequently observed to be a consequence of paternal or ancestral affiliation. However, it is doubtful whether family ties or family considerations are nearly as important determinants as the fact that we *first* become familiar with the beliefs and the defenses of the beliefs of our family [34, p. 191].

The primacy effect could also be a factor in determining the outcome of opinion changes following debates. In such situations the conditions for the operation of primacy are closely approximated, since one side first presents its position and then the second side offers a view in direct opposition to that of the first. Elaborate precautions to counterbalance the order effects would be required in order to equalize the persuasive potentiality of the two sides.

Of even greater concern would be conditions for equitable administration of justice. In the presentation of court cases it is generally the rule that the prosecution presents its case and the defense follows. If the law of primacy is operative, we would find a constant bias in favor of the prosecution's position, since it always has the advantage of first position.

While the lawyer of the plaintiff is reviewing his case and making his appeal, the belief of the jurors is already in the process of formation, and they are not to be dissuaded from their position by an equal amount of evidence or persuasive appeal on the part of the defendant's lawyer, according to the law of primacy [34, p. 191].

Scientific Implications

While there are practical implications derivable from many of the studies in this volume, the "applied" utility of the research is secondary. The factor motivating the present studies has been the opportunity afforded by research in this area to examine some of the basic theoretical problems involved in the process of influence and persuasion. It will become evident from the different chapters what a variety of theoretical issues are involved in the relatively straightforward problem of order of presentation. Thus Hovland, Campbell, and Brock use this framework for a better understanding of the process of commitment to a particular point of view, a factor which increases one's resistance to subsequent influence. A comparison is made between the type of commitment involved in an anonymous and in a public statement of one's position. Social psychological factors of commitment could be said to interact with the problem of order of presentation, since there may be a tendency in many primacy-recency situations to respond with a committing type of action after hearing only one side of an issue.

Luchins utilizes order of presentation to analyze the phenomenon of "set" in a communications framework. He finds many points of similarity between the persistence in personality studies of impressions created by the first material presented and the persistence of set in problem-solving situations (30). Luchins attempts to use the principles derived from some of his earlier studies of set (or "Einstellung") in problem-solving in order to eliminate primacy effects in personality judgment.

A theory of "cognitive need" is employed by Cohen to interpret the effects of different orders of motivational appeals and informational material. In utilizing this type of formulation he is able to relate the problem of order to the personality characteristics of the recipient. He compares individuals with high interest in understanding (high cognitive needs) with others whose interest in understanding is low and easily satisfied with only superficial comprehension.

McGuire utilizes a stimulus-response theory of learning to analyze the effect of order of presentation in the communication-persuasion process. His prediction from the theory is that when a series of communications, some desirable to the recipient and others undesirable, are to be transmitted, it will be more effective for the desirable to precede the undesirable than to reverse the order. He regards the communicator (or source) as a stimulus to which an agreement response can be conditioned. This response is the final unit in a chain of responses (like attending, comprehending, etc.) intervening between the initial stimulus and the response of agreement with the source. When the desirable messages are communicated first, the intervening and final responses are followed by reward and hence conditioned to the stimulus, but when the undesirable ones are first, no reward follows and extinction of these responses is to be expected.

The Janis and Feierabend experiment may be cited as a final example of the manner in which important aspects of psychological theory may be tested within the framework of organization of communications. These authors see an opportunity for analysis and extension of theories of conflict in the setting of order of arguments within a communication (Appendix B). They view positive ("pro") and negative ("con") arguments in a communication as placing the recipient in an approach-avoidance type of conflict, wherein the positive arguments motivate him in the direction of accepting the communicator's position (approach behavior) while the negative arguments motivate him to reject these recommendations (avoidance behavior). Two methods of influencing this conflict are compared: strengthening approach tendencies before exposure to the avoidance-producing influence, and the reverse order, in which avoidance tendencies are established before the approach tendencies are consolidated.

It will be seen from the foregoing discussion that various authors explore the problem of order effects from different theoretical positions. This diversity is probably characteristic of a newly developing field such as social psychology. But it is anticipated that ultimately the many diverse phenomena analyzed in the present studies will be encompassed within a single unified theory. It will also be noted that although over a dozen different experiments are reported, the problems of even this highly delimited field are far from solved and many interesting further explorations immediately suggest themselves. It is hoped, however, that the present studies will serve to stimulate interest in these problems and to suggest some of the ways in which theoretical and applied issues may be jointly attacked.

PART ONE

Order Effects in
Successive Communications

CHAPTER 2

Is There a "Law of Primacy in Persuasion"?[1]

CARL I. HOVLAND AND WALLACE MANDELL

IN THE EXPERIMENT by Lund (34) mentioned in the preceding chapter written arguments were presented successively for and against an issue, with the affirmative arguments presented first for half of the subjects and the negative first for the remaining subjects. Opinion questionnaires were filled out by the subjects before the presentations and again after the first and after the second communications. The change resulting from the first communication was greater than the change brought about by the second communication, and Lund described this outcome as the Law of Primacy in Persuasion. Directly opposed results were reported in a later study by Cromwell (7), in which speeches presented in second position had a greater influence on the attitude of the listeners than those presented first.

One possible explanation for the disparity in the results

1. A preliminary report of the experiments was presented to the Eastern Psychological Association meeting in 1952 (35) and a brief mention of the results appears in *Communication and Persuasion* (18).

from the two studies may lie in the different evaluation procedures they employed. In the Cromwell study the effects of the two communications were evaluated after both sides had been presented. In the Lund study, on the other hand, one of the questionnaires was administered immediately after the first side had been presented. This may have had the effect of requiring the subjects to review the arguments, formulate their own conclusions and put their position "on record" after reading only one side of the issue. Thus the measurement process might have had the effect of "freezing" opinion and of causing individuals to be less likely to change their opinions once they had committed themselves on a questionnaire. Lund mentions this possibility: "the students, *having committed themselves* after the reading of the first discussion, *will remember this rating* and will tend to be influenced by their desire to be consistent when asked to make another rating after reading the opposed discussion" (34, p. 190).[2] Since commitment on the questionnaire is extraneous to primacy itself, if it were an explanatory factor Lund's results might thus really be attributable to the effect of the measurement process rather than to sequence effects.

The present experiment had as its original purpose the evaluation of "formulation-commitment" as a factor responsible for the appearance of primacy in Lund's experiment and its absence in Cromwell's. Lund's experiment was repeated, but with an additional group in which the subjects were not asked for their opinion until after both sides had been presented. A second objective, which turned out to be of greater interest, was to determine the generality of the results obtained by Lund.

2. Italics ours.

Experiment I

Procedure. Every effort was made to follow Lund's procedures as closely as possible. The questionnaire, of the same
type that Lund used, was administered by the instructor two
days in advance of the communications.

The list of propositions, such as "Should all men have
equal political rights?" was presented accompanied by a
scale of belief which ran from +10 (Belief allowing for no
doubt) to —10 (Disbelief allowing for no doubt). Subjects
were instructed to check the number corresponding to the
extent to which they felt inclined to affirm or deny the validity of the proposition. Two of the topics found to be most
effective by Lund were used for the communications:
"Should all men have equal political rights" and "Is the protective tariff a wise policy for the United States." His material
was mimeographed and presented to the subjects to read. Ten
minutes were allowed for the reading of each side.

Counterbalancing was employed, so that half of the subjects began with the affirmative version and half with the
negative. The "Lund Repetition" group was given the rating scale for belief after the first side had been read, while
this step was omitted for the other group. Both groups were
given the belief scales after both versions had been read.

This experiment was done at Hofstra College and Columbia University on a series of undergraduate psychology
classes. Twelve classes were employed in this experiment,
ranging in size from 14 to 51 students. One class was used for
each of the four main conditions on the "equal rights" issue,
while the remaining subjects were used for two replications
of the "tariff" issue. A total of 357 students was studied.

Results. The results from Experiment I are presented in Table 1.

TABLE 1. *Mean Belief Ratings before and after Communications (Experiment 1)*

		LUND REPLICATION CONDITION		NO INTERVENING QUESTIONNAIRE	
		Affirmative First	*Negative First*	*Affirmative First*	*Negative First*
TOPIC I. "EQUAL RIGHTS"		N = 26	N = 27	N = 21	N = 16
Before communications	(a)	5.12 (d)	4.18	(a) 5.24 (d)	4.94
After first side	(b)	6.65 (e)	4.75		
After both sides	(c)	5.92 (f)	5.17	(c) 3.29 (f)	1.88
Effect *		−0.19 (Recency)		+1.11 (Primacy)	
		p = .77		p = .28	

TOPIC II. "PROTECTIVE TARIFF"

First Replication

		Affirmative First	*Negative First*	*Affirmative First*	*Negative First*
		N = 14	N = 16	N = 28	N = 27
Before communications	(a)	2.00 (d)	0.69	(a) 1.85 (d)	1.70
After first side	(b)	4.71 (e)	1.00		
After both sides	(c)	2.64 (f)	1.50	(c) 3.37 (f)	3.30
Effect		−0.17 (Recency)		−0.08 (Recency)	
		p = .85		p = .89	

Second Replication

		Affirmative First	*Negative First*	*Affirmative First*	*Negative First*
		N = 47	N = 51	N = 33	N = 41
Before communications	(a)	−0.26 (d)	0.71	(a) 1.52 (d)	0.41
After first side	(b)	2.23 (e)	−0.86		
After both sides	(c)	0.17 (f)	0.04	(c) 2.18 (f)	0.41
Effect		+1.10 (Primacy)		+0.66 (Primacy)	
		p < .01		p = .21	

* Advantage of first position $= (c − a) − (f − d)$. If value is positive, data show primacy; if negative, recency. The complete formula for advantage of first position is $[(b − a) + (d − e)] − [(b − c) + (f − e)]$ but b's and e's are common terms and hence cancel.

The mean ratings for belief derived from Lund's scales are shown for the repetitions of Lund's experiment and for the additional groups which were not given the belief scale between the first and second communication. Under the conditions originally used by Lund only one of the groups shows primacy ($p < .01$), the other two showing insignificant recency effects. When the opinion questionnaire is omitted after the first side is presented, two of the groups show primacy and one recency. These effects are small and nonsignificant. The omission of the intervening questionnaire does not have any consistent effect: it increases the amount of primacy for one topic and decreases it for the other. But in neither case is the difference statistically significant. The absence of consistent primacy effects of the type obtained by Lund overshadows the problem of the effect of the intervening questionnaire, since the latter is only significant when relevant to the explanation of primacy effects.

Experiment II

In view of the absence of clear-cut primacy effects in the first experiment it was thought desirable to obtain more data on a straight repetition of the Lund condition, using topics of possibly greater current interest. Hence a second experiment was conducted.

Procedure. In this experiment new communication materials dealing with the issues "Anti-histamines should be sold without a prescription" and "An atomic submarine is feasible at the present time" [3] were mimeographed. Two days before the communications were presented, the instructors administered an opinion questionnaire concerning these issues. A seven-point rating scale for degree of belief was em-

3. This study was done in 1949, when this was a much-debated topic.

ployed. The communications were administered so that one issue was used for each class. Within each class counterbalancing led to half of the subjects reading the positive argument first, while half read the negative first. In addition to the before and after questionnaires, half of the classes took the same questionnaire between the two communications. The time for reading and instructions was the same as in the first experiment.

This experiment was done at New York University on a series of 10 psychology classes. On the first topic the groups totaled 56 and 60 subjects, while for the second there were 37 and 38 students. Thus the total number of subjects was 191.

Results. The data from this experiment were analyzed in a manner analogous to that of Lund and of the first experiment by determining the mean degree of belief in the propositions discussed in the communications. The data are presented in Table 2. Again we find an absence of evidence for primacy under our conditions. Three of the groups exhibit recency effects, one at a statistically significant level ($p < .01$). Only one of the four groups showed evidence of primacy and this was only significant at the .08 level.

Discussion

The present findings raise serious doubts as to the generality of the results obtained by Lund (34). For only two of the seven groups run under his conditions did we find primacy effect, and only one of these was statistically significant. The remaining five groups showed a greater effectiveness of the second communication, although only one of the differences was of sufficient size to be statistically significant ($p < .01$). While Lund's own results support the operation of primacy, he does not give tests of significance to indicate the extent of reliability of his difference. If his variability was of the same order of magnitude as ours, it is unlikely that

TABLE 2. *Mean Belief Ratings before and after Communications (Experiment 2)*

		Affirmative First		Negative First
TOPIC III. ATOMIC SUBMARINES				
First Replication				
		N = 39		N = 41
Before communications	(a)	4.87	(d)	5.12
After first side	(b)	4.62	(e)	4.88
After both sides	(c)	4.12	(f)	5.00
Effect		—0.63 (Recency)		
		p < .01		
Second Replication				
		N = 17		N = 19
Before communications	(a)	4.53	(d)	3.96
After first side	(b)	4.48	(e)	3.11
After both sides	(c)	3.83	(f)	3.42
Effect		—0.41 (Recency)		
		p = .10		
TOPIC IV. ANTI-HISTAMINES				
First Replication				
		N = 18		N = 17
Before communications	(a)	3.77	(d)	2.94
After first side	(b)	4.66	(e)	3.23
After both sides	(c)	4.16	(f)	3.53
Effect		—0.20 (Recency)		
		p = .67		
Second Replication				
		N = 20		N = 20
Before communications	(a)	2.95	(d)	3.00
After first side	(b)	4.85	(e)	3.05
After both sides	(c)	4.25	(f)	3.45
Effect		+0.85 (Primacy)		
		p < .08		

more than one of his three groups would show a statistically significant effect (his typical group contained approximately 20 subjects).

If there is a significant difference in outcome between our experiment and that of Lund, what variation in conditions may have been responsible? In terms of the analysis presented in *Communication and Persuasion* we would seek differences either in the conditions of *learning* or of *acceptance*. With respect to the former, the most likely difference between the two experiments would be in the subjects' motivation to learn. In the Lund study the experimenter was presumably the subjects' regular classroom instructor. Under these conditions one would expect that the motivation to learn the first-presented communications would be derived from previous classroom experiences in which the material presented by the teacher had to be learned, later formed the basis for a test, etc. This would provide strong motivation for learning the first communication. When the teacher then proceeded to reverse his stand, the subjects may have wondered what was happening. They may have suspected that they were being used as guinea pigs in an experiment. As a result of the changed conditions, motivation to learn the second communication might have dropped and consequently less careful attention paid to this second communication. Such conditions would produce a primacy effect (i.e. a greater impact exerted by the first communication than by the second).

This same set of conditions may also have influenced *acceptance* of the communication. Lund's students may have accepted the first communication as being implicitly "sponsored" by the instructor. The subsequent advocacy of an opposed point of view could have aroused their suspicion and reduced their confidence in the communication. Since they were unaware of being experimental subjects at the time that they filled out the first questionnaire, their opinions may have been influenced by the first communication. The adverse effects would become apparent on the second questionnaire and result in reduced effectiveness for the second communication.

In our study the experimenter was not the teacher but rather someone from outside of the school presenting rival views on the issue. It is our belief that these conditions are more typical of situations to which research findings are likely to be applied than are those of Lund. Thus in communications involving debates, rival political candidates, or court-room alternation of prosecution and defense, the presentations are clearly labeled as opposing points of view and do not secure acceptance of the first material on the basis of classroom conditions of motivation and acceptance. An interesting study in which different orders of presentation of prosecution and defense arguments are compared is reported by Weld and Roff (42). Calculations by us based on their data indicate recency effects.

Another difference may be the degree of commitment involved in the two studies. The set of results bearing on the extent of opinion change with and without intervening questionnaire makes it appear unlikely that merely expressing one's opinion privately on a questionnaire will significantly influence one's subsequent position on the issue. But in Lund's experiment there may have been some expectation on the part of the subjects that their answers would be read by the experimenter (teacher), and this may have increased their tendency to give consistent answers and hence produced primacy effects.

It appears, then, that primacy is not an easily reproducible phenomenon but may occur only under a certain set of conditions. Hence it is probably premature to postulate a universal law of primacy. Another limitation of generality must be mentioned. Under the artificial and controlled conditions involved in the present experiments, as well as in Lund's original study, there is some assurance that subjects are at least exposed to each side of the issue. Even then there is great variability in outcome. But under naturalistic conditions choice of exposure is controlled by the communicatee, and hence still other factors will operate to determine which side of the issue is perceived by the subject. Studies show that under these conditions subjects tend to expose themselves only to those communications whose point of view is sympathetic to their own (27, 28). Certainly in such cases a universal law of primacy is not likely to apply, and even should primacy effects obtain, different mechanisms would probably mediate their operation.

CHAPTER 3

The Effects of "Commitment" on Opinion Change Following Communication [1]

CARL I. HOVLAND, ENID H. CAMPBELL, AND
TIMOTHY BROCK

ONE OF THE EXPLANATIONS which may be advanced for a possible greater effectiveness in persuasion of that side of an issue which is presented first is that the recipient often carries out actions after hearing the first side which make him more resistant to subsequent persuasion. One type of action frequently involved is the statement of one's own opinion to others after hearing only one side of an issue. "Once we have committed ourselves we frequently dare not change our position lest we be challenged with our former statements" (34, p. 190). Apparently the response of answering a questionnaire anonymously, however, is not capable, by itself, of producing this type of effect, as has been shown in the preceding chapter. The failure of a private commitment to produce a primacy effect suggests either that per-

1. A preliminary report of the first of the two experiments described in this chapter was given at the American Psychological Association meeting in 1954 (15). The assistance of Mr. Raymond C. Smith in preparing the scripts for the talks is gratefully acknowledged.

sonal commitment does not in fact produce such an effect or that the type of commitment presented was not strong enough to produce a change. The purpose of the present study, accordingly, was to investigate further the role of commitment in the primacy-recency problem by introducing a stronger form of "commitment." The prediction was made that an individual required to state his position publicly after being exposed to a communication will tend to retain this position in the face of a subsequent communication on the opposite side of the issue. He will maintain this first position to a greater extent than will a control group which does not commit itself after hearing only the first side. The effect of this influence would thus be to produce a greater primacy effect in the commitment group than in the control group.

Experiment I

Procedure. The over-all plan of the study was to present successively two communications on opposite sides of the same issue, separated in time by the experimental conditions of commitment or noncommitment. The topic of the communications was "The reduction of the legal voting age to 18 years—the current draft age." One communication was strongly in favor of the change and the other strongly in favor of retaining the present voting age of twenty-one years.

The communications were presented to four groups, two experimental and two control, in a balanced order. One experimental and one control group received the communications in an affirmative-negative order, while the other experimental and control group received them in the negative-affirmative order. The communications were delivered by four speakers, each of whom gave one communication twice, once to an experimental group and once to the corresponding control group. Any single group would, therefore, hear the two opposing points of view coming from two different individuals.

Opinions on the issue discussed were measured one week before the experimental session, and twice during the experiment. One of the latter measures was taken after the first communication and one after the second.

Subjects. The subjects were 98 pupils in a senior high school in New York City. They were attending the summer sessions of the school, either to make up work in courses which they had failed the previous year, or to take special classes which would advance their standing. They were divided into four groups—two experimental and two control —equated on the basis of the results of the opinion questionnaire given one week before the experimental session. The purpose of the assignment to groups was to insure that each group should have approximately the same number of students who were initially for, and initially against, the proposed change.

The commitment. In selecting a form of commitment for the present experiment, it was decided to use a procedure which would essentially be a public affirmation of individual opinion, yet not involve any of the social interactions which usually accompany a public expression of opinion—such as discussions, and reactions of approval and disapproval. This was accomplished (a) by asking all of the groups (both control and experimental) in the study to write a short paragraph presenting their own frank opinions on the issue after the first communication, and (b) by telling the subjects in the commitment groups that their opinions would be published in a PUBLIC AFFAIRS PAMPHLET to be circulated in their schools where teachers and classmates would read them. To increase the credibility of this publication, the subjects were shown a printed page from another pamphlet of the same organization. The subjects were further cautioned to read over their statements to be sure that this was the form in which they wanted them printed, and above the space for the signature the following reminder appeared: "Sign your name here as you wish it to appear under your printed statement." The control or "noncommitment" groups, in contrast, were to write a similar essay but were told instead that their papers would be kept anonymous, and were asked not to sign their names under their opinions.

Through the use of this technique, it was hoped to control the practice variable but still to provide differential motivation for the two groups. It was expected that the subjects who were asked to sign their opinions and were told that they would be published would deviate less from their written commitments under the impact of the second communication than would the control group. After the experiment the purpose of the study was fully explained to the subjects.

The opinion measures. The initial opinion measure was given to the students by the high school faculty one week before the main experimental session. It consisted of a single item concealed in a general questionnaire which was presented to the subjects as a survey of the listening habits of Americans to determine the impact of radio and television on their knowledge and opinion of current events. The key item was stated as follows:

The voting age should be reduced from 21 years to the draft age of 18 years.

   _____ Agree strongly

   _____ Agree somewhat

   _____ Neither agree nor disagree

_____ Disagree somewhat
_____ Disagree strongly

The second opinion measure was the "commitment" or control activity. These written statements of opinion (described above) were rated on the same scale used in the pretest questionnaire and in the final opinion measures. Three independent judges scored each subject's written statement using the above questionnaire item as a guide. The medians of the three judges' ratings for each subject were then calculated and used as the second opinion measure.

After the essays were written, the experimenter said that some of the students had expressed a desire to hear the other side of the argument and that accordingly another speaker has been secured who would present the case for the opposed position. This constituted the second communication.

The final opinion measure was a second questionnaire administered immediately after the second communication. This questionnaire included the previously described key item on voting age as well as a number of unrelated questions.

Results. The principal results of this experiment are shown in Table 3. The data support the hypothesis in showing that the groups receiving the commitment procedure were less influenced by the subsequent communication than were the control groups. Thirty-five per cent of the control group subjects were influenced in the direction of the second communication, while only 16 per cent of the group who had committed themselves earlier were influenced in this direction. The net difference in per cent of subjects changing positively is significantly greater for the control than for the experimental group ($p < .05$, one tail).

Inspection of the results suggest another possible effect which was not anticipated but is consonant with the same theoretical explanation. This is a slight but not significant tendency for the experimental group to be changed less by

TABLE 3. *Percentage of Subjects Showing Changes in Opinion Following Communication Presented* AFTER *Commitment Procedure*

(Experiment I)

	Commitment Group (N = 49) per cent	Control Group (N = 49) per cent
1. Changes in direction of communication	16	35
2. Changes in opposed direction	10	10
3. No change	73	55
Net change (1–2)	+6	+25

p < .05 (one tail)

the first communication than the control group. Results on the per cent of the subjects who change their opinion after the first side is presented are given in Table 4. There is an

TABLE 4. *Percentage of Subjects Showing Changes in Opinion Following Communication Presented* PRIOR TO *Commitment Procedure*

(Experiment I)

	Commitment Group (N = 49) per cent	Control Group (N = 49) per cent
1. Changes in direction of communication	22	35
2. Changes in opposed direction	20	22
3. No change	57	43
Net change (1–2)	2	13

p = not signif. (two tails)

11 per cent difference in net proportion of changers for the two conditions, but this does not reach statistical significance with a two-tailed test.

Experiment II

In the preceding experiment the effect studied barely reached statistical significance and there was one possible imbalance which could have affected the outcome. One of the speakers appeared to have a better reception than the others. There was spontaneous applause following his talk. Hence, it was felt desirable to repeat the experiment on another group. Following some further exploration it also appeared desirable to try to increase the strength of the commitment without modifying the requirement that the effect not be mediated by knowledge of group opinion or by verbalization. It was thought that a more powerful commitment could be achieved by having the individual present his opinion for a publication seen by his own group and in the immediate future.

Procedure. Except for the change in commitment procedure all details were the same as in Experiment I. The commitment was produced by telling the subjects in the experimental group that their opinions would be printed in the high school newspaper which was to be circulated to the student body the following week. The speakers who presented the affirmative and negative communications were previously equilibrated for effectiveness. Sixty-nine junior and senior high school students at a high school in Madison, Connecticut, served as subjects.

Results. Data comparable to those presented in Table 3 for Experiment I are shown in Table 5 referring to responses to the communication following the commitment procedure.

The effects are again statistically significant and have the same implication. Because of the greater control of speaker effectiveness in the second experiment there can be greater confidence in the outcome. Incidentally, we found that the

TABLE 5. *Percentage of Subjects Showing Changes in Opinion Following Communication Presented* AFTER *Commitment Procedure*

(*Experiment II*)

	Commitment Group (N = 35) per cent	Control Group (N = 34) per cent
1. Changes in direction of communication	14	41
2. Changes in opposed direction	11	9
3. No change	75	50
Net change (1–2)	3	32

p < .03 (one tail)

effect of commitment on change following the first communication was again present but still not to a significant extent. Analysis showed that the net proportion of subjects changing in the direction of the communication was 15 per cent for the control group but only 6 per cent for the commitment group.

Discussion

The predicted reduction in the effect of the second communication under commitment conditions is confirmed, but much further research remains to be done to determine the factors which facilitate or minimize commitment effects. Some information, mostly in line with common-sense notions about the topic, is provided by our pre-test experience. In one of the pilot studies for the replication, the same two speakers were used as in the final replication, with the same commitment induction used for Experiment I, i.e. subjects were told that at a later time their answers would be printed in some magazine. The commitment was thus rather indefinite. No significant effects of this procedure were obtained on opinion change. Only with the procedure involving almost immediate publication in a newspaper printed by and for their friends and classmates did clear-cut commitment effects occur. In this connection it is worth recalling that mere private commitment, in terms of filling out an anonymous questionnaire, does not appear to have any decisive effect on any of the issues studied to date (Hovland and Mandell, Chap. 2, above). In a recent study by Deutsch and Gerard (8) only one of their private commitment procedures was effective, and this they attribute to "faulty experimental procedure" such that subjects "in the first self-commitment variation perceived the commitment situation as though it were a public commitment" (p. 633).[2] On the other hand, in a study by Bennett (3) private commitment was as effective as public. It should be stressed that in the present studies no attempt was made to have the subjects regard their expression of opinion as a commitment.

Our results appear to highlight the importance of socially mediated rewards. When the individual knows that his name and opinion will be circulated among his close friends in a short time, he probably rehearses his position in preparation for the imminent publicity in such a way that he becomes

2. It is interesting to note that Fisher, Rubinstein, and Freeman (12) interpret the results of Deutsch and Gerard as suggesting that private commitment produces more influence than public commitment. Deutsch and Gerard themselves say: "it is apparent that this internally sustained influence to conform with one's own judgment was not as strong as the combination of external and self-motivated influences" (12, p. 634).

resistant to countercommunication. Changing one's position under these circumstances is difficult, since to do so means to relinquish the basis upon which the individual has developed anticipations of desirable social interaction and attention which usually accompany the public expression of an opinion. An individual's close daily associates expect him to behave in a consistent and reliable manner. Under such circumstances an individual who contemplates revocation of a position he has publicly maintained may well anticipate some disparagement and negative social reinforcement from his associates if his attitude change becomes known to them. When the change in attitude remains anonymous, these effects are much less clear-cut. But there are still many individuals who will have internalized to the extent that they respond to imagined disapproval in the same way that most individuals do to direct social interaction related to their maintenance of position. Such individuals will be expected to show commitment effects even on an anonymous questionnaire. But the effects will be smaller and a smaller proportion of the population will be so influenced.

CHAPTER 4

Primacy-Recency in Impression Formation

ABRAHAM S. LUCHINS

THE PRESENT INVESTIGATION is concerned with evaluating the effects of various kinds and sequences of information communicated about an individual on the impressions formed concerning that person's personality and nature. The information is in the form of a written communication describing an individual's behavior during the day. Some of the communications consistently portray one behavioral pattern, but others are inconsistent in the sense that the first half portrays one behavioral pattern and the second half a different pattern. The inconsistent communications permit the study of whether the impressions which arise tend to give equal weight to both halves or to be influenced more by the first half (primacy effect) or the second half (recency effect).

A well-known study on the role of primacy in impression-formation by Asch (1) showed that the order in which a list of trait-names was presented apparently influenced the impression gained of the person to whom the traits referred. There are many real-life judgment situations wherein a person's traits are not explicitly delineated but in which the traits attributed to the person are inferences drawn from observations of his behavior or from other information about him. Our study does not begin with discrete traits; rather, we use descriptions of a person's behavior, and we are interested in whether the order in which the descriptions are presented will influence the inferences made about the individual. In addition to obtaining information about the operation of primacy and recency, the present study attempts to throw some light on the nature of reactions to inconsistencies or contradictions within the communication.

Method

The material employed consisted of mimeographed paragraphs describing someone named Jim. One paragraph, reporting rather friendly, outgoing behavior will be referred to as the extrovertive or E description (Jim-E). This paragraph is as follows:

> Jim left the house to get some stationery. He walked out into the sun-filled street with two of his friends, basking in the sun as he walked. Jim entered the stationery store which was full of people. Jim talked with an acquaintance while he waited for the clerk to catch his eye. On his way out, he stopped to chat with a school friend who was just coming into the store. Leaving the store, he walked toward school. On his way out he met the girl to whom he had been introduced the night before. They talked for a short while, and then Jim left for school.

Another paragraph, which will be referred to as the introvertive or I description (Jim-I) reports Jim as behaving in a somewhat more withdrawn manner in situational contexts similar to those of the E communication. The I paragraph is as follows:

> After school Jim left the classroom alone. Leaving the school, he started on his long walk home. The street was brilliantly filled with sunshine. Jim walked down the street on the shady side. Coming down the street toward him, he saw the pretty girl whom he had met on the previous evening. Jim crossed the street and entered a candy store. The store was crowded with students, and he noticed a few familiar faces. Jim waited quietly until the counterman caught his eye and then gave his order. Taking his drink, he sat down at a side table. When he had finished his drink he went home.

Two other descriptions were obtained by combining the E and I descriptions. When the E description is immediately followed by the I description, without a paragraph indention between the two, we refer to it as the EI sequence. When the I description is immediately followed by the E description, without a paragraph indention, we refer to it as the IE sequence. It should be kept in mind that the EI and IE communications differ only in the temporal order of the two blocks of information from which they are constructed; the two are identical with respect to the sentences they contain and the order of these sentences within each block. For ease of exposition, we refer to the EI or IE sequence as combined or inconsistent information and to the E or I description as consistent information or as an isolated block.

The experiment was introduced with the following words: "In everyday life we sometimes form impressions of people based on what we read or hear about them. You will be given a paragraph about someone named Jim. Please read the paragraph through only once and then answer the question (or questions) about Jim."

S then received a mimeographed booklet, the first page of which contained a description of Jim with the test questions (or question) on subsequent pages. All answers were to be written in the booklet. When the experiment was administered to a group, subjects were asked not to make any oral comments but to write on the blank left-hand pages of the booklets any remarks they might want to make. When it was administered to one individual at a time, the experimenter recorded comments made by the subject but did not answer any questions other than to repeat the instructions.

A subject is said to belong to Group E, Group I, Group EI, or Group IE, depending on whether he received the E, I, EI, or IE description, respectively. Groups E and I constitute the control groups and Groups EI and IE the experimental groups.

We are interested in whether subjects who received the combined information were influenced equally by both blocks or whether they were influenced more by one block than by another. In each experiment, responses that are judged to be based predominantly on information in the E block are labeled as E responses, responses that are judged to be based predominantly on information in the I block are labeled as I responses, and responses that reflect the equal influence of both blocks are labeled as BOTH responses. The greater influence of the lead block is considered indicative of primacy; the greater influence of the second block, of recency.

In order to study whether the obtained group trends support primacy or recency, in each experiment we apply two indices:

Index 1: Percentage E responses in Group EI minus percentage E responses in Group IE. A positive number reveals primacy (since it means E responses are more predominant when the E block is given first than when it is given second), and a negative number reveals recency.

Index 2: Percentage I responses in Group IE minus percentage I responses in Group EI. Here, too, a positive quantity signifies primacy (since it means that I responses are more predominant when the I block is given first than when it is given second), and a negative quantity signifies recency.

EXPERIMENT 1 [1]

The experiment was group administered to 16 classes in New York City schools, half of them at the high school and the others at the college level. All of the members of one class received the same description of Jim. There was a total of 437 subjects in this experiment, with 117, 113, 91, and 116 in Groups E, EI, IE, and I, respectively.

Half of the control groups were asked to select the item in the following list which most adequately described Jim: (a) friendly, (b) unfriendly, (c) none of these. Most subjects in the college class, as well as in the high school class, which received the E description chose the adjective *friendly* (93 and 96 per cent) while the corresponding classes receiving the I description predominantly chose the adjective *unfriendly* (84 and 80 per cent).

The remaining control groups were asked to choose from the following list: (a) friendly, (b) shy, (c) none of these. Again the predominant response was the term *friendly* for Jim-E (97 and 94 per cent) while most of those who read about Jim-I selected the term *shy* (88 and 92 per cent). Less

1. Grateful acknowledgment is made to Aaron Weiss for assistance in collecting and tabulating the data used in Experiment 1.

than 4 per cent of any Group E selected the term *unfriendly* or *shy* while less than 4 per cent of any Group I ever selected the term *friendly*.

The findings thus reveal a very decided tendency to describe Jim-E as friendly and Jim-I as unfriendly or shy. For this reason, the rating of *friendly* was labeled as an E response and that of *unfriendly* or *shy* as an I response.

The next step was to ascertain reactions to combinations of the E and I descriptions. Half of the experimental groups were asked to select the item in the following list which most adequately described Jim: (a) friendly, (b) unfriendly, (c) more friendly than unfriendly, (d) more unfriendly than friendly, (e) equally friendly and unfriendly. In the remaining groups each subject had a list similar to this one except that the term *shy* had been substituted throughout for the term *unfriendly*.

Selection of either category *a* or *c* was scored as an E response, since it gave predominance to the "friendly" characteristic and therefore suggested that greater weight had been given to the E block. Choice of either category *b* or *d* was scored as an I response since it gave predominance to the "unfriendly" or "shy" characteristic and therefore suggested that the I block had exerted the more dominant influence. Choice of category *e* was labeled as BOTH, since presumably both blocks of information had been equally influential.

Results

Failure to respond. It might have been expected that after reading the EI or IE sequence, with its rather inconsistent information, subjects would perhaps be unable to rate Jim in terms of the available friendly-unfriendly or friendly-shy classifications. It was found, however, that failures to respond were relatively low in the experimental groups, ranging from 0 to 9 per cent, with a mean of 5 per cent. In the control groups, failures to respond (in which we include choice of the category "none of these") ranged from 0 to 13 per cent with a mean of 7 per cent. Differences in percentages of "no response" between groups were not statistically significant.[2]

Responses indicative of equal influences of both blocks. Relatively few subjects contributed responses which suggested that equal weight had been given to both blocks of information. Percentages of BOTH responses ranged from 7 to 10 per cent with a mean of 6 per cent in Group EI and ranged from 12 to 15 per cent with a mean of 13 per cent in Group IE. Differences between the two groups were not statistically significant.

Primacy-recency. Failures to make a selection, and selections reflecting the equal influence of both blocks of information, accounted together for only about 15 per cent of the 204 experimental group subjects' responses. In other words, about 85 per cent of their responses were made in terms of one block or the other. The number of E and I responses and the extent of primacy or recency in terms of the two indices described above are given for the four groups in Table 6. Coll.–F (H.S.–F) refers to the college (high school) classes that received the friendly-unfriendly ratings, and Coll.–S (H.S.–S) to the college (high school) classes that received the friendly-shy ratings. For all four groups studied, each of the two indices pointed to primacy, to the greater influence of the lead block. Each of the differences is statistically significant. While there were some subjects who showed recency effects, on the

2. Unless otherwise specified, differences will be described as not statistically significant if they failed to meet the .05 criterion; differences will be described as significant if they met the .01 criterion.

whole primacy prevailed over recency, regardless of whether the E or the I block came first. An extremely large primacy effect is clearly shown.

Examination of Table 6 reveals that as we go from Groups E to EI to IE to I, the percentage of E responses decreases and

TABLE 6. *Survey of Results in Experiment 1*

	PER CENT E RESPONSES				PER CENT I RESPONSES				PRIMACY-RECENCY		
	E	EI	IE	I	E	EI	IE	I	Index 1 *	Index 2 **	Mean
Coll.–F. (N = 122)	93	75	17	3	3	11	63	84	+58	+52	+55
H.S.–F. (N = 109)	96	86	27	3	4	11	50	80	+59	+39	+49
Coll.–S. (N = 99)	94	70	12	4	6	15	68	88	+58	+53	+55
H.S.–S. (N = 107)	97	82	15	0	0	7	70	92	+67	+63	+65
Total	95	78	18	3	3	11	63	86	+60	+52	+56

* Per cent E responses in EI group minus per cent E responses in IE group.
** Per cent I responses in IE group minus per cent I responses in EI group.

the percentage of I responses increases. The ranking positions also indicate that E responses and I responses to the isolated blocks of information consistently serve as upper and lower bounds for responses to the combinations of the blocks. For E responses, the E block serves as the upper bound and the I block as the lower bound. For I responses, the boundary roles are reversed, with the I block now serving as the upper and the E block as the lower bound.

EXPERIMENT 2

Indicants of primacy effects in Experiment 1 were based on responses to only one task. This perforce gave a limited picture of the subjects' impressions of Jim. In the hope of obtaining a more comprehensive picture of these impressions, we used a number of tasks. After reading the communication, each subject was asked to write a paragraph conveying his impression of Jim. We were interested in whether subjects' willingness to do so, and the content of submitted paragraphs, would reflect the nature and sequence of the information received. It also seemed important to ascertain whether the different communications exerted differential effects on recall. Accordingly, sentences were given to be completed on the basis of what had been read. A great variety of rating tasks was also included. The questionnaire, which was the same in all booklets, was as follows:

1. Please write a paragraph of about 25 words giving your impression of Jim, the individual about whom you have just read. In other words, write what you think of Jim based on the information you just obtained.

Will you select from each of the following the word or phrase that, in your opinion, best fits Jim? Put a line under your selection.

2. (a) friendly; (b) more friendly than unfriendly; (c) more unfriendly than friendly; (d) unfriendly; (e) equally friendly and unfriendly.

3. (a) forward; (b) more forward than shy; (c) more shy than forward; (d) shy; (e) equally forward and shy.

4. (a) social; (b) more social than unsocial; (c) more unsocial than social; (d) unsocial; (e) equally social and unsocial.

5. (a) aggressive; (b) more aggressive than passive; (c) more passive than aggressive; (d) passive; (e) equally aggressive and passive.

Complete each of the following on the basis of what you read about Jim.

6. In the store, Jim _____

7. With his fellow students, Jim _____

8. When Jim saw the girl he had met the night before, he _____

To allow for more careful observation during the experiment and for more intensive questioning after it, it was administered individually, or to small groups of from two to six subjects, rather than to classroom groups, as had been the case in the previous experiment. All subjects were students attending colleges located in Montreal, Canada. Ten experimenters (student assistants) worked independently of each other in collecting the data for the experimental groups. There was a total of 350 subjects, of whom 40 received the E description, another 40 the I description, 135 the EI sequence, and another 135 the IE sequence.

Analysis of Results

Student assistants served as judges of responses to the questionnaire. The judge did not know the particular communication which the subject had read. The score of NONE was assigned to an item if the subject had failed to answer it. The written sketch submitted by the subject was compared, through content-analysis, with the information contained in the E and I blocks. The findings of this analysis, taken in conjunction with the picture of Jim conveyed to the judge by the sketch, determined the scoring. The sketch was scored as E+ (or as I+) if it was decidedly in line with the E (or the I) block, as E— (or I—) if it seemed to be based mainly but not solely on the E (or the I) block, and as BOTH if it seemed to be influenced equally by both blocks. For the rating tasks, E+ was assigned to the choice of phrase *a* (friendly, forward, social, aggressive), E— to phrase *b* (more friendly than unfriendly, etc.), I— to phrase *c* (more unfriendly than friendly, etc.), I+ to phrase *d* (unfriendly, shy, unsocial, passive), and BOTH to phrase *e* (equally friendly and unfriendly, etc.). A sentence-completion task was scored as E+ (or I+)

if the sentence had been completed on the basis of precisely the relevant behavior described in the E (or the I) block, as E— (or I—) if there was some modification of the information but not sufficient to change the essential idea involved, and as BOTH if it was completed in terms of the relevant actions contained in both the blocks. An item was scored as IRRELEVANT if the response did not fit any of the other scoring categories. We calculated the percentage of a group's total opportunities to respond that fell into each of the scoring categories.

Separate analysis was carried out for each of the following: E+ responses, I+ responses, E responses (the sum of E+ and E— responses to a test task), and I responses (the sum of I+ and I— responses to a test task). Consistently, E+ responses revealed the same trends as E responses and I+ responses as I responses. We shall therefore deal with E and I responses and not with their components.

Results

Failure to respond and irrelevant responses. Did the combination of the E and I blocks, with the differing behavioral patterns attributed to Jim, make it difficult for subjects to develop an impression of Jim which could be conveyed in a written sketch? Of the 350 subjects in all groups, only one failed to write a paragraph in response to the first task. Most of the sketches involved paraphrasing of parts of the communication, with a sprinkling of adjectives and occasional value judgments. Some of the paragraphs seemed unrelated to the communication and were scored as IRRELEVANT. But the percentage of IRRELEVANT sketches was not higher after the combined information than after the isolated blocks. Similarly, percentages of NONE and IRRELEVANT scores in the remaining tasks were not higher in the experimental groups than in the control groups.

The largest proportion of failures to respond occurred in Group E with reference to the rating task involving the forward-shy characteristics. Apparently unwilling to rate Jim-E in terms of these characteristics, 40 per cent of the subjects in Group E failed to make a selection in this task. In general, failures to reply were somewhat higher for the rating tasks, which were multiple choice, than for the remaining tasks, which were open-ended. For the questionnaire as a whole, the mean percentages of NONE and IRRELEVANT scores for Groups E, EI, IE, and I, respectively, were:

% NONE: 8, 7, 8, 2
% IRRELEVANT: 4, 4, 5, 8

Differences between group means were not statistically significant for either type of score.

Responses giving equal weight to both blocks. Following an isolated block, responses scorable as BOTH were found only in the rating tasks. For example, 20 per cent of Group I rated Jim-I as "equally friendly and unfriendly." Following the combined information, some responses scorable as BOTH were given to every task. One-fifth of each of Groups EI and IE wrote paragraphs which suggested equal influences of both blocks. Responses scorable as BOTH were less frequent in the subsequent tasks. We are particularly interested in whether the sentences were completed in terms of information contained in both blocks (e.g. "First he stopped to talk to the girl but later he crossed the street when he saw her"). On the average, only 11 and 13 per cent of Groups EI and IE, respectively, completed the sentences in terms of both blocks of information. For the questionnaire as a whole, the mean percentages of responses scored as BOTH were 2, 8, 8, and 6 per cent for Groups E, EI, IE, and I, respectively. Again, differences between group means were not statistically significant.

Primacy-recency effects. NONE, IRRELEVANT, and BOTH scores together accounted for only about one-fifth of each group's total opportunities to respond. This means that about four-fifths of the response opportunities in each group yielded replies which showed that one block was more persuasive than the other. We applied the same two indices of primacy-recency used in Experiment I to each of the eight items in the questionnaire. The percentages of E and I responses to each task after the various communications and the indices of primacy-recency are presented in Table 7.

TABLE 7. *Survey of Results in Experiment 2*
(*N: Group E, 40; Group EI, 135; Group IE, 135; Group I, 40*)

	% E RESPONSES				% I RESPONSES				PRIMACY-RECENCY*		
	Group				Group				Index	Index	Mean
Item	*E*	*EI*	*IE*	*I*	*E*	*EI*	*IE*	*I*	*1*	*2*	*Mean*
Written impression	88	41	20	0	0	24	49	82	+21	+25	+23
Friendly-unfriendly	90	71	54	25	0	19	31	55	+17	+12	+15
Forward-shy	50	33	17	0	0	51	67	95	+16	+16	+16
Social-unsocial	85	60	46	5	0	30	41	85	+14	+11	+13
Aggressive-passive	55	26	18	5	45	55	62	75	+8	+7	+8
Sentence *re* store	93	58	30	12	0	19	41	62	+28	+22	+25
Sentence *re* students	88	63	34	8	0	23	44	77	+29	+21	+25
Sentence *re* girls	97	59	29	3	0	19	46	87	+30	+27	+28
Total questionnaire	80	51	31	7	6	30	48	77	+20	+18	+19

* Indices same as in Table 6.

It will be recalled that if an index of primacy-recency yields a positive difference, it points to primacy, whereas if it yields a negative difference, it points to recency. Table 7 indicates that all of the differences are positive, thereby testifying to the predominant influence of the first block. All differences are statistically significant.

Awareness of Conflict

Did subjects who received the combined descriptions regard the two blocks as conflicting with one another? There were a few subjects in Groups EI and IE (but none in Groups E or I) who, while reading the communication or immediately after finishing it, told the experimenter or wrote in their booklets that more than one person was involved in the communication, that two distinct Jims were being described. Some of them added that they could not answer the questionnaire for both Jims. But such spontaneous comments were relatively infrequent; usually subjects did not spontaneously reveal that they were aware of or troubled by conflicting data.

Further attempts to investigate awareness of contradictions led to questioning of 70 subjects (half of them in Group EI, half of them in Group IE). At the close of the experimental session each of these subjects was asked, "Did you notice any contradictions or inconsistencies in the material about Jim which you read?" Answers to this question (written by those tested in small groups but given orally by those tested individually) did not differentiate between those who had received the EI sequence and those who had received the IE sequence. Of the 70 subjects, 37 reported that they had noticed contradictions or inconsistencies, 10 failed to answer the question, while 23 claimed that they had *not* been aware of any contradictions or inconsistencies. It is difficult to know whether these answers reflect what actually occurred during the reading of the communication; the answers do suggest that subjects may have differed in their degree of awareness of inconsistencies.

The second question asked of the 70 subjects was: "How did you reconcile contradictions or inconsistencies in the material about Jim which you were given to read?" A few subjects who previously claimed not to have noticed contradictions now wrote how they had reconciled the (unnoticed?) contradictions. Of the 37 subjects who had given affirmative answers to the first question, three said they had not been able to reconcile the contradictions on the basis of the available information, 17 said that they had successfully reconciled the apparent inconsistencies, while the answers of the 17 remaining subjects implied that the contradictions had not been sharp enough to require reconciliation or that they had not been sufficiently troubled by the contradictions to worry about them.

Thus 40 out of the 70 subjects reported either not noticing inconsistencies or not being disturbed by them to the point where an active attempt at integration was necessary.

Among the replies given by those who said they had reconciled the inconsistencies were the following: Jim is essentially a friendly person and when he appeared to act in an unfriendly manner it was because he was tired, or because he had an unhappy day at school, or because the girl was a bore. Jim is friendly except with new people whom he does not know well and Jim was new in the neighborhood, or the people whom he did not stop to talk to were new, or were not well known to Jim. Jim is very selective in making friends. Although Jim is an outgoing fellow who likes people, there are times when he needs solitude and wants to be left alone. Jim is awkward with girls and needs to mix more. Jim acts differently at different times because he is at an awkward stage of development or because he is an adolescent, a moody person, a "nervous person," "a queer fellow," or a "strange character." Unfortunately we do not know whether subjects developed these lines of reasoning while reading the communication or while answering the questionnaire, or whether they spun them to order only when questioned at the end of the session.

EXPERIMENT 3

The third experiment was performed in order to explore further the limits of influence of each communication, as reflected both in the types of questions subjects were willing to answer about the person described and in the types of answers which they gave. It touches on the question of the kind of inferences which will be drawn following various forms of knowledge about a person, an area in which there has been relatively little research. A new questionnaire was devised (below, pp. 187–9), covering a broader realm than the questionnaires used in the previous experiments and pertaining to aspects of the described person which had not been explicitly dealt with in the communications. In addition to tasks involving the writing of a paragraph to convey the impression, ratings, and sentence-completions, the present questionnaire asked the subject to list adjectives which he thought were applicable to Jim; asked him if he liked Jim; asked questions about Jim's physical features and expressive behavior; asked him what Jim thought of himself, his parents, teachers, and boys and girls of his own age; and described a variety of situations in which the subject's task was to predict Jim's behavior.

The experiment was administered individually or to small groups of from two to six subjects. Five student assistants worked independently of one another in helping to collect the data. The 264 subjects were high school seniors and college lower classmen in Montreal, Canada, with 44 receiving the E block, another 44 the I block, 87 the EI sequence, and 89 the IE sequence.

Analysis of Responses

The response to the first task (paragraph submitted by the subject) was scored as in Experiment 2. It was classified as E (or I) if it seemed to reflect the predominant influence of the E (or the I) block of information; as BOTH if it reflected equal influences of the two blocks; and as IRRELEVANT if the sketch did not fit the above classifications. The classification of NONE was used if S did not respond to the first task.

Since we lacked an a priori basis for determining what should constitute an E (or I) response to some of the remaining items of the questionnaire, we adopted the following criteria. In each task a reply was classified as E only if this reply, or responses similar to it, had been made by at least 20 per cent more subjects in Group E than in Group I (with the difference significant at the .05 level of confidence), and had *not* been made by the majority of subjects in Group I. A reply was classified as I if the roles of Group E and Group I were interchanged in these conditions. The classification BOTH was used when a subject gave an E as well as an I response to an item. The classification of NONE was used if he failed to respond or if he selected the choice category "none of these." A reply was scored as IRRELEVANT if it did not fit any of these classifications.

Results

Concerning NONE *scores.* It is of interest to see whether subjects were willing to reply to the questionnaire, many items of which were in an area which transcended the specific information contained in the communications. There were some subjects who, during or after the experimental session, protested apropos of some of the items, "How am I supposed to know this?" or words to this effect. But such comments were infrequent. The quantitative data also reveal a general willingness to respond.

Regardless of which communication was received, subjects usually responded to the different kinds of items in the questionnaire. As in the previous experiment, the rating tasks (the only tasks of a multiple-choice character) yielded somewhat more NONE scores than the other tasks. For each type of task and for the total questionnaire, intergroup differences in percentages of NONE scores were small and not significant. The 264 subjects in all groups showed a mean percentage of only 3 per cent NONE scores for the total questionnaire.

Differentiating items. Responses to each of 25 items of the questionnaire (out of the total of 35 items) differentiated sufficiently between Group E and Group I to meet the criteria established for E as well as for I scores. It may be remembered that a criterion for classifying a reply as E or as I was that differences between Groups E and I be statistically significant at the .05 level of confidence; in actual fact, the differences on 24 of the 25 items proved to be significant at or beyond the .01 level.

The score of E was found to apply when the subject supplied one or more of the following adjectives or synonyms for them: sociable, social, friendly, outgoing, popular, likable, happy, extrovert; when he reported that he liked Jim, that he thought Jim was likable; when he predicted that Jim would accept the party invitation, stop to talk to Harry's friends, accept the camp counseling position, celebrate his acceptance into medical school with a party, offer an idea to start a class discussion, take action to prevent domineering behavior toward him in the science club, voice disagreement with the lecturer, and protest if the barber overlooked his turn; when he described Jim as well developed, muscular, or athletic; having an average rate of speech; walking erectly or with good posture or with a quick or medium gait; thinking of himself as the equal of others or as an average person; being interested in girls; being interested in or liking boys his own age; when he rated Jim as friendly or more friendly than unfriendly, as forward or more forward than shy, as social or more social than unsocial, as aggressive or more aggressive than passive; and when he completed a sentence in terms of the relevant behavior contained in the E block or minor modifications of this behavior.

The score of I was found to be applicable when the subject applied one or more of the following adjectives or synonyms for them: shy, reserved, quiet, lonely, unpopular, unfriendly; when he reported that he did not like Jim, did not think him likable; when he said that Jim would not accept the party invitation, would not stop to talk to Harry's friend, would accept the office job, would not make a party when accepted into medical school, would not offer an idea for class discussion, etc.; when he described Jim as having average or underaverage body build, or as being thin, weak, slight, or spindly; of having a slow rate of speech; walking slowly or with poor posture; when he reported that Jim would feel himself inferior to other people, dislike or be shy of girls, and dislike or not be interested in boys his own age; when he rated Jim as being unfriendly or more unfriendly than friendly, as shy or more shy than forward, as unsocial or more unsocial than social, as passive or more passive than aggressive; and when he completed a sentence in terms of the relevant behavior described in the I block or minor modifications of this behavior.

Responses giving equal weight to both blocks. Responses scored as BOTH were relatively infrequent. Paragraphs that received this score were submitted by 9 per cent of Group EI and 6 per cent of Group IE. About one-fifth of the subjects in each of these groups offered adjectives, some of which were of an E and others of an I character. Only 1 per cent of the sentence-completion tasks in Group EI, and also in Group IE, were completed in terms of the actions contained in both blocks. No other task in Group EI or IE yielded responses classified as BOTH. Replies made by subjects of Groups E or I never fell into the BOTH classification.

Primacy-recency. For the total of 25 differentiating items, NONE, BOTH, and IRRELEVANT scores together accounted for only 7, 12, 10, and 11 per cent of the response opportunities in Groups E, EI, IE, and I, respectively. This means that about nine-tenths of the response opportunities in each group reflected the sole or main influence of one block of information. In order to determine whether group trends reflected the predominant influence of the first or second block, we applied the two indices of primacy-recency used earlier. The percentages of E and I responses after the various communications, together with the indices of primacy and recency are presented in Table 8 for each of the 25 differentiating items.

Table 8 shows a positive index (indicative of primacy) for all but one of the 25 differentiating items, the one referring to body build. The over-all difference was 19 per cent (the same as in Experiment 2). When the various groups' percentages of E (or of I) replies to an item are ranked according to size, it is found that the groups tend to maintain the same ranking positions throughout.

Awareness of conflict. A sample of subjects who had received the inconsistent communications were personally interviewed. They were asked if they had noticed inconsisten-

TABLE 8. *Survey of Results in Experiment 3*
(*N: Group E, 44; Group EI, 87; Group IE, 89; Group I, 44*)

Nature of Task/Group	% E RESPONSES				% I RESPONSES				PRIMACY-RECENCY *		
	E	EI	IE	I	E	EI	IE	I	Index 1	Index 2	Mean
Written impression	87	41	10	0	0	36	81	83	+31	+45	+38
Adjectives	73	50	26	3	0	30	54	97	+24	+24	+24
Do you like Jim?	87	82	65	37	10	14	32	57	+17	+18	+18
Is Jim likeable?	93	82	78	47	7	14	20	50	+4	+6	+5
Party invitation	97	80	65	30	3	17	32	67	+15	+15	+15
Met Harry's friends	73	56	51	13	27	34	46	87	+5	+12	+8
Employment choice	93	56	29	7	7	39	66	93	+27	+27	+27
Medical school party	63	46	36	10	37	51	63	87	+10	+12	+11
Discussion idea	93	60	42	27	7	36	57	83	+18	+21	+20
Science club	67	46	30	27	27	49	66	73	+16	+17	+17
Lecturer	63	32	21	23	37	64	74	77	+11	+10	+10
Barber shop	80	49	32	17	20	41	64	80	+17	+23	+20
Body build	57	15	11	7	27	67	63	77	+4	−4	0
Manner of walk	73	56	44	20	20	26	42	53	+12	+16	+14
Rate of speech	47	41	21	20	27	36	40	47	+20	+4	+12
Thinks of himself	87	60	36	30	0	25	57	67	+24	+32	+28
Thinks of girls	77	67	35	17	13	18	51	50	+32	+33	+32
Thinks of boys	93	56	30	33	7	21	46	53	+26	+25	+25
Friendly-unfriendly	97	77	56	13	0	18	37	53	+21	+19	+20
Forward-shy	60	21	6	7	20	64	93	87	+15	+29	+22
Social-unsocial	97	59	34	3	0	36	60	87	+25	+24	+25
Aggressive-passive	53	28	10	7	20	57	76	73	+18	+19	+19
Sentence *re* store	67	32	25	7	27	40	57	73	+7	+17	+12
Sentence *re* students	93	58	42	3	0	31	45	93	+16	+14	+15
Sentence *re* girl	100	60	26	0	0	27	69	100	+34	+42	+38
Total of 25 items	79	52	34	16	14	36	56	73	+18	+20	+19

* Indices same as in Table 6.

cies in the communication. Over one-third reported that they had not; close to another third said that they had noticed some slight discrepancies in the descriptions; and the remainder said that they had been aware of inconsistencies or contradictions in behavior. When asked how they had reconciled the inconsistencies, most subjects who reported inconsistencies said that they had been too slight to require reconciliation; others said that they had accounted for the inconsistencies by appealing to differences in mood, tiredness, surroundings, previous occurrences, adolescent awkwardness with girls, etc.; and the minority claimed that they had not been able to reconcile the contradictions. (The reactions were similar to those of subjects in Experiment 2.) When attempts to reconcile the two blocks were reported, they usually revealed that the first block was taken as portraying the "real" Jim while the subsequent information was regarded as describing behavior which had to be explained away. These qualitative results corroborate the quantitative data by suggesting that the characteristic reaction to inconsistencies, when they were noticed, was to pay greater heed to the earlier behavior.

DISCUSSION

The trend toward primacy. One of the striking features of the findings was that in each experiment primacy was more pronounced than recency. How can we account for this trend? Why did the first block tend to have a more dominant influence than the second? A few subjects offered their own explanations. These were the few who, upon noting contradictions in the communications, decided explicitly to respond on the basis of the first block. An extreme case is furnished by one subject who wrote, "Two distinct Jims are being described. I can't answer the questionnaire for both so I'm going to answer only for the first Jim described." Such comments, however, were very infrequent. The majority of subjects did not explicitly indicate that they were going to answer in terms of only part of the communication. Even for the subject whose comment was just cited, there still remains the question of why he decided to respond in terms of the "first Jim" and not in terms of the "second Jim."

Attempts to account for primacy may appeal to what is known about serial learning. In the literature on learning, the terms "primacy effects" and "recency effects" denote the well-known phenomenon that items at the beginning and end of a series tend to be learned better than the items in between (cf. 16). But whether or not it is appropriate to invoke serial effects in accounting for our results is a moot issue. Subjects were not actually told to learn or memorize the communication. However, the results hint that subjects tended to learn better, or at least to retain better, information contained toward the beginning of the communication rather than toward the end (if one judges, for example, by responses to the sentence-completion tasks). For some subjects, differential learning of the information toward the beginning and end of the communication may have occurred and may have influenced responses to the questionnaire; in these cases the results may be said to reflect a supremacy of primacy over recency in social learning.

One may also appeal to what is known about interference phenomena in learning. The combined descriptions resemble the typical interference design (18). Learning of the second part may have been interfered with by the previous learning of the first part with primacy a consequence of this interference.

It seems apparent that subjects probably did not face both blocks in the same manner. The first block introduced Jim to the subject. While he was reading the second block he was already under the influence of what he had read before, and this may have interfered with his learning of, or colored his interpretation of, the second block. If the subject was aware of contradictions between the two blocks, he may have been puzzled or confused while reading the second block. In short, subjects probably faced the first block with more of an open mind and with less interfering influences than was the case for the second block.

There is also the possibility that the subject paid more attention to the first block, precisely because it was first. He needed some information about Jim; having obtained some, he may have read the remainder more rapidly or more carelessly, perhaps just scanning it or not reading it at all. That the background was similar in the two blocks may have helped to foster the belief that it was sufficient to skim or that the second part was less important since the subject already knew how Jim behaved in such situations. Those who assumed that Jim (or any other individual) is necessarily consistent in his behavior, or that one can readily and validly generalize about him from a segment of his behavior, may have been more prone to pay greater attention to the first part. What they needed was some information about Jim; once they derived the information from the beginning of the communication they may have regarded the remainder as less important, as elaborations of the previous information, or as rather superfluous. (It should be emphasized that this is speculation on our part. When some subjects were specifically questioned on this score, the prevalent response was that in reading they had been equally attentive to all parts of the communication.)

Some subjects apparently *accepted* the first part of the communication more readily than the second. After being introduced to Jim, so to speak, in the first part they were in a position to be more critical of the second part. Comments made by some subjects suggest that they regarded the beginning of the communication as portraying the real Jim, the "essential nature" of Jim, while toward the end of the communication came information which had to be explained away.

In short, factors of learning, attention, and acceptance may all have played roles in making the first block more efficacious than the second.

It seems to us that a parsimonious explanation for primacy-recency and for the prevalence of primacy, can be found in the concept of "set" and, in particular, in the concept of "Einstellung." (cf. 30) We postpone development of the Einstellung hypothesis until the next chapter, which presents experiments that are outgrowths of this hypothesis.

Individual differences in primacy-recency. There were considerable variations in the extent and consistency with which subjects were influenced by the first or second block. One wonders what kind of individual differences played a role in determining why one subject consistently showed primacy effects, another showed recency effects, and yet another did not show either of these responses consistently. Individual differences might be accounted for in terms of propensity for developing a set or for recovering from a set, of rigidity or flexibility, of tendencies toward closure, of tendencies toward "Prägnanz" (making for a regular, stable impression and working against irregularities or inconsistencies), of tolerance of ambiguities, etc.

The nature of the communication. An interesting question is whether the trend toward primacy effect is a resultant of the particular kinds of communications that were used. The communications were *read* by the subjects. What would happen to primacy-recency if the subject were to hear the communication read to him or played as a recording, or if he saw the behavior described in the communication enacted before him in a moving picture?

The communications described a *person.* It should prove of interest to use descriptions of nonhuman objects, scenes, and events in order to see what happens to primacy-recency effects.

The two blocks which comprised the combined description were similar in their background or situational contexts. Against similar backgrounds, Jim behaved in different ways, as portrayed in the two isolated communications. Research has been initiated to discover what happens to primacy-recency when the backgrounds of the two blocks are not so similar. Other needed studies involve use of more pronounced inconsistencies and the use of inconsistencies which are interspersed throughout the communication rather than confined to differences between two blocks.

Role of the questionnaire: impression versus expression. It is recognized that the responses the subject makes to the questionnaire may not necessarily reflect his actual impression of Jim; that is, overt expression of the impression may not be isomorphically related to the impression itself.

It is also a point worth stressing that the particular questions which are asked may influence the answers obtained.

They may influence not only the subject's overt expression but even the very impression obtained.

The impression, *as aroused by the communication,* need not necessarily be well organized, nor need it cover all the aspects involved in the questionnaire. But the aroused impression might be so labile that, under the pressure of the specific probing, it could be modified, extended, elaborated, made less nebulous and more clear cut, and brought to bear on a wide variety of factors pertaining to Jim. At the same time the impression aroused by the communication must be sufficiently directive to exert an influence on the continuing process of impression formation, if one is to judge by differences in response after the various communications.

An alternative explanation is also feasible. The impression may be thought of as a range of possibilities of responding, with the range structured or subdivided in such a way that the individual would be likely to react to (or to report upon) certain aspects in spontaneous expression, to other aspects when he was asked to give a general impression, and to still others under specific probing. The range may have different aspects or facets, some of which the subject may not be explicitly aware of until he is asked to face them.

In short, the impression as aroused by the communication may have inherent in it the various facets later brought out by the specific questions or it may have suggested or fostered influences that prompted certain answers. In any event, it seems patent that the questionnaire was an important determinant of the manner in which the subject portrayed Jim. The role of a particular test item may have been to help organize the impression, or to make explicit information that was previously inherent in the impression but of which

the subject had not been aware or which he had not expressed. Or an item may have had the role of emphasizing an
aspect of the impression or of inducing elaborations, exten-
sions, and modifications of, or inferences from, the impression.

Important methodological problems for future research are
those of assessing as accurately as possible the actual impression aroused by the communication; of determining whether
spontaneous expression is most revealing of the impression
and whether a description written by the subject is more
revealing than specific questioning; whether open-end questions are better than multiple-choice tasks; and, more generally, of studying the kind of questions to ask, and the order
in which they should be asked to minimize discrepancies between impression and expression.

Implications for impression formation. The typical subject's willingness to reply to the various items of the questionnaire may have involved, in the experimental situation,
the same tendency to classify and categorize people which
one experiences in everyday life. To the extent that the
present findings are applicable to life situations, they suggest that an individual having only limited information
about another may nevertheless be willing to draw a variety
of inferences concerning a second individual and to make
judgments, predictions, and assessments in areas wherein he
lacks specific information. The results further suggest that
the nature of the (limited) information possessed, the degree
of consistency of behavior in the sample he is acquainted
with, and the order in which he received the information
may influence his subsequent judgments and his recall of the
person's actions. Since the group trends point toward primacy, they suggest that the earlier information (or the first

"contact" with Jim) was more influential than the later information. The results would thus seem to support the adage about the importance of "first impressions."

The experimental design, perhaps not too far removed in some respects from the typical case of forming impressions of personality on the basis of what one reads or hears about another person, is con iderably further away from what happens in impressions involving direct contact with people. Life situations do not typically bring an unbroken sequence of information about the person; nor does a confirming series tend to be followed by a nonconfirming series. In the research situation we give him specific questions to answer. Moreover, the answers he gives have no actual consequences for the judged and the judge, nor for others, whereas in life situations there may be consequences. Finally, in life situations the actual interaction between the judge and the judged and their social perceptions may themselves influence the impression and its expression. What are needed are studies of impression formation in the laboratory which more exactly duplicate aspects of lifelike situations, as well as investigations of impressions formed in the course of daily living. Such studies may help us to know how widespread and how lasting are primacy effects, as well as what influences are exerted on the initial and subsequent impressions by the kind of information received.

CHAPTER 5

Experimental Attempts to Minimize the Impact of First Impressions

ABRAHAM S. LUCHINS

EXPERIMENTS described in the previous chapter revealed a trend toward primacy, that is, a tendency for the first part of a combined communication to be the more influential. Could factors be introduced experimentally into these communications to weaken or eliminate the primacy effect? Our attempts to do so were modeled after some of the experimental efforts to minimize "Einstellung" effects in problem-solving situations (30, 32). We conjectured that the primacy observed was in the nature of an Einstellung,[1] a conjecture suggested by certain similarities between the organization of the communications and the organization of a series of volume-measuring problems used in studying Einstellung effects.

The series of problem-solving tasks, involving measure-

1. "Einstellung" is a term introduced by German psychologists to describe a tendency to persist in a general type of activity and difficulty in changing over to a very different type of activity. It is frequently used synonymously with the English word "set" (cf. 30).

ment of volume, begins with several problems which are similar in appearance, all of which may be solved by one (rather complex) method. They are followed immediately by further problems, also similar in appearance, which may be solved by the oft-repeated method but also by simpler, more direct methods. Many subjects showed Einstellung effects, in that they utilized the oft-repeated method in solving the test problems while overlooking the more direct methods of solution.

A parallel may be drawn between the first block of the combined communication and the set-inducing problems. Just as the problems are homogeneous in nature, similar in appearance and in pattern of solution, so the first block of information is homogeneous in nature, consisting of a series of described actions all of which imply one pattern of behavior. The second block is in some respects similar to the test problems. The latter are linked to the set-inducing problems by their both being volume-measuring problems and by the homogeneity of the temporal sequence in which the two sets are presented. Likewise, the second block of the communication is closely linked to the first by their both pertaining to Jim and by the homogeneity of the temporal sequence in which the subject perceives them. Similarity of situational contexts in the two blocks may also have contributed to the apparent unitary nature of the communication.

In problem solving, the problems in the first part of the series tended to foster a directional tendency such that test problems were viewed from the frame of reference of the earlier set-inducing problems. Analogously, the first block may have fostered a characteristic way of conceiving of Jim, or may have directed and channelized thinking about Jim or a way of viewing the communication. Individuals receiving the set-inducing problems often neglected, or were seemingly blind to, the direct methods of solving the subsequent test problems. Analogously, subjects who received the combined descriptions may have neglected, or even been blind to, information in it and interpretations of it which were recognized by subjects who received the second block of information alone.

Efforts to minimize Einstellung effects in the volume-measuring problems met with some success. When an explicit admonition against the development of a set or Einstellung was given at the outset, prior to the series of problems, somewhat less Einstellung effect was obtained. Such an admonition was even more effective if placed immediately after the set-inducing problems and just prior to the test problems. Most successful of all in reducing the Einstellung effect was the interpolation of certain tasks between the set-inducing and test problems. Qualitative data suggest that the effectiveness of an admonition or an interpolated task in weakening Einstellung, was directly related to its success in breaking the apparent unity of the series, in making the subject view the test problems as separate from the set-inducing problems.

The experiments to which we now turn are concerned with the effect upon primacy of issuing an explicit warning against primacy effect just prior to presenting the combined communication, of interpolating this warning between the first and second blocks of information, or of interpolating certain tasks between the two blocks.

Procedures

Each S received a mimeographed booklet containing a communication (or communications) about Jim. Subsequent pages of the booklet held the long-form questionnaire (reproduced below, pp. 187–9) used in Experiment 3 of the previous chapter.

Group 1 (standard conditions). The procedure was described in detail in the preceding chapter. The introductory instructions, the same as in the preceding experiments, were as follows:

"In everyday life we sometimes form impressions of people based on what we read or hear about them. You will be given a paragraph about someone named Jim. Please read the paragraph through only once and then answer the questions about Jim."

For half of the subjects, the first page of the booklet contained the EI communication and for the others the IE communication. A maximum of two minutes was allowed for reading of the EI or IE sketch. In this experiment, as well as in all the others, the subjects were allowed as much time as they desired for completion of the questionnaire.

Group 2 (prior warning). The booklets and the introductory instructions were identical with those used for Group 1. However, after the introductory instructions, the experimenter remarked:

"People are inclined to form an opinion of a person during the first few minutes of acquaintance with him and often this opinion may be held throughout their acquaintance, regardless of later actions by the person which contradict this impression."

A minute or two was allowed for discussing the fact that first impressions often carry over and influence subsequent perceptions of an individual. The experimenter then said that in everyday life it is of value to suspend judgment about an individual until we have seen him in many situations. He concluded with these remarks:

"I want each of you to try to suspend judgment of the individual about whom you are to read until you have completely finished reading all that is written about him. Don't make any snap judgments. Take into account all that you read."

The subjects then read the EI or IE sketch and answered the questionnaire.

Group 3 (interpolated warning). The first page of the booklet used for this group contained only the E block of information for half of the subjects and only the I block for the others. The introductory instructions were the same as for Group 1 except that the last sentence was, "Please read the paragraph through only once and then place the booklet face down on your desk and await further instructions." One minute was allowed for reading of the first block. After that came the supplementary remarks and discussion used for Group 2. Following the admonition against a snap judgment, subjects were told to turn to the second page of the booklet. This contained the other block of information. A maximum of one minute was allowed for reading it before subjects turned to answer the questionnaire on subsequent pages. Thus the procedure used for this group differed from that for the previous one in that (a) the booklet did not contain the E and I blocks on one page in an unbroken sequence but instead the blocks were separate paragraphs on successive pages, and (b) the admonition and related remarks used with Group 2 were interpolated between the two blocks of information rather than being given in advance.

Group 4 (interpolated number-task). The booklets and the introductory instructions were the same as for Group 2 but the interpolation between the blocks was different. One minute was allowed for reading of the first block. Then new paper was distributed and simple number-tasks were given, involving the addition, subtraction, and multiplication of numbers. After about five minutes had been spent on these number-tasks, subjects were told to turn to the second page of the booklet. A maximum of one minute was allowed for reading of the second block of information before subjects responded to the questionnaire.

Control group.[2] The instructions were the same as for Group 1. For half of the group, the first page of the booklet contained the E block while for the others it contained the I block. The questionnaire followed.

Subjects

The subjects were 300 students in a high school in Montreal, Canada. Each experimental treatment was administered to small groups of subjects in a study hall of the high school. There was a total of 60 subjects in each experimental group and in the control group.

For Group 1 through 4, the half of the group receiving the EI communication (or the E block before the I block) constitutes the EI group; the other half the IE group. In the control group, the half of the subjects receiving the E communication constitutes the E group; the other half the I group.

Expectations

If primacy effects are in the nature of Einstellung effects, and if factors which seemed to weaken the Einstellung in the volume-measuring problems are similarly effective with regard to primacy in the communications, we might expect to

2. The control group subjects were students in the same school as the subjects in the present Groups 1 through 4. They were included in the control group used in Experiment 3 of Chapter 4.

find less primacy effects for Groups 2, 3, and 4 than for Group 1. Moreover, if the introduced factors follow the pattern of relative efficacy shown by similar factors in weakening Einstellung in the volume-measuring problems, we might expect primacy effects to decrease from Groups 1 through 4.

Analysis of Results

Each protocol was scored by a student assistant who did not know the particular communication or experimental procedure that the subject received. To simplify the scoring, it was limited to the 25 items which had differentiated between Groups E and I in Experiment 3 of the preceding chapter. (These same items also differentiated between the present control groups.) A response was scored as E or as I if it (or a very similar response) had been so scored in Experiment 3 of the preceding chapter. It was scored as NONE if the subject failed to respond or selected the "none of these" category. To simplify the presentation of results, all other responses were labeled as OTHER.

Results

Responses scored as NONE or as OTHER were relatively infrequent. The mean percentage of responses of various kinds in Groups 1 through 4, respectively, were:

% NONE:	9,	6,	8,	7
% OTHER:	6,	6,	8,	13
% E:	40,	36,	41,	40
% I:	45,	52,	43,	40
% E + % I:	85,	88,	84,	80

It is seen that responses scored as E or as I together accounted for four-fifths or more of the response opportunities in each group.

Mean effects. The two indices of primacy-recency described in Chapter 4 were applied to the mean percentages of responses made to the total set of 25 items, with the results shown in Table 9. As before, a positive number indicates a

TABLE 9. *Primacy-Recency Effects for Groups 1–4 in Terms of Mean Responses*
(30 Ss in Group EI and 30 in IE for each experimental treatment)

Experimental Treatment	% E resp. EI (1)	IE (2)	% I resp. IE (3)	EI (4)	Primacy-Recency (1–2)	(3–4)	Mean
1. Standard	49	31	60	30	+18	+30	+24
2. Advance warning	37	35	54	49	+2	+5	+4
3. Interpolated warning	38	43	40	47	−5	−7	−6
4. Interpolated task	32	48	34	45	−16	−11	−14

primacy, and a negative number a recency, effect. It will be seen that there is a progressive decrease in primacy and increase in recency as we go from Group 1 to Group 4. Both indices are significantly positive in Group 1. In Group 2 (advance warning) smaller primacy effects are observed. The picture is very different for Group 3 (interpolated warning), where recency effects now make their appearance. Still stronger recency effects are indicated by Group 4.

Individual test items. The two indices of primacy-recency were applied to the response to each of the 25 test items for each of the four groups (Table 10). It will be seen that the

TABLE 10. *Primacy-Recency Effects for Groups 1–4 in Terms of Percentages of Test Items*

Experimental Treatment	% E items showing Primacy	Recency	% I items showing Primacy	Recency	Mean % items showing Primacy	Recency
1. Standard	76	8	96	0	86	4
2. Advance warning	44	32	48	40	46	36
3. Interpolated warning	20	56	32	52	26	54
4. Interpolated task	16	76	24	64	20	70

picture is much the same as for the total set of items, with the percentage of test items showing primacy decreasing progressively from Group 1 to 4, while the percentage of items indicating recency increases. For the first two groups more of the items are indicative of primacy effect; for the last two more show recency effects.

Both tables then give consistent evidence that the percentage of primacy effect is substantially reduced by the introduction of warning and by interpolated activity. Thus the trend from Group 1 to 4 is exactly in line with the trend predicted on the basis of results in the volume-measuring problems previously investigated. For Groups 3 and 4 the experimental procedure not only eliminated primacy effects but actually brought about greater than chance expectancy of recency effects.

Discussion

The relative efficacy of various factors in weakening primacy. The interpolated warning and the interpolated number tasks were more effective in weakening primacy than the advance warning. In the light of findings from the volume-measuring problems, it is plausible that the greater success of an interpolation (whether of an admonition or of number tasks) was due to the break it created between the blocks and the consequent decreased likelihood of the communication being perceived as a homogeneous unit.

Primacy effects were less discernible after the number tasks. Perhaps this was because the number tasks were not related to the communication and therefore made for a sharper break between the two blocks than did the warning, which was concerned with the communication. The facts that new papers were distributed and that the subjects engaged in solving the number tasks on these new papers may have contributed to a more marked hiatus between the blocks, which in turn may have operated against the communication being perceived as a homogeneous unit. Moreover, the five minutes allotted to the number tasks was longer than the time spent on the intervening warning, and this, too, may have emphasized the break between the blocks (cf. also 31).

In order to explore the effects of time intervals, two new experiments were conducted in the same high school using new subjects. In one experiment an interval of five minutes was allowed between the two blocks, with the time spent on a lecture on a topic of history delivered by the classroom teacher. In the other experiment an interval of 17 minutes was allowed between the two blocks, with the time also spent on a history lecture. Half of the subjects in each experiment had the IE sequence, and the others the EI sequence. Analysis of responses to the questionnaire showed that the experiment with the five-minute time interval yielded results similar to those for Group 4, where five minutes had been spent on arithmetical tasks. The experiment with the 17-minute interval yielded even more recency effects. These results highlight the need for systematic investigation of the influence of various time intervals (and of what happens during these intervals) on primacy-recency.

Another provocative problem for research is to attempt to minimize the totality of primacy and recency effects. The closest we came to minimizing the combined total of such effects was with Group 2 using the advance warning. One wonders what would happen to the totality of primacy and recency effects if subjects were warned, either prior to the combined communication or between the blocks, against *both* primacy and recency.

It is conceivable that some degree of primacy or recency may be inevitable by virtue of the nature of the combined communications and the fact that it pertains to a person. We usually think of a person as having a characteristic organization (personality, character) from which his behavior stems. A person is usually conceived of and perceived as a unity of some sort and not as an "and-summation" of actions. It is implicit in the initial instructions and explicit in the first question that the subject's task is to describe Jim as a person —that is, to abstract a "person" from the instances of behavior he has read. But the subject may not be able to abstract a person if he gives equal weight to both blocks. If the subject is to see Jim as one person (and not as two distinct individuals), and if he is to see the kind of characteristic organization from which Jim's behavior stems, it may be necessary for him to emphasize one block of behavior at the expense of the other, to make one central and the other peripheral in the impression. The subject may be aware of giving greater emphasis to one block (e.g. as were the subjects who regarded one block as revealing the "real Jim" and the other as containing actions to be explained away) or he may not be aware of this. But conceivably, the very process of forming an impression may favor an emphasis on one block.

Moreover, the nature of the questionnaire itself may favor an emphasis on one block. If the subject follows closely the information in the communication and gives equal weight to both blocks, he may at best be able to say that Jim is changeable, inconsistent, or that he behaves differently at different times. To answer the questionnaire by giving equal weight to both blocks would mean that the subject would fail to answer some questions and would have to give conditional or equivocal answers to other questions. For example, in the prediction questions he might answer that Jim would behave one way or another depending on his mood. But if the subject considers that the assignment calls upon him to give decisive answers, he may not be satisfied with (or even consider) such equivocal responses. In short, perhaps the closest the subject can come to fulfilling the assignment of describing Jim while still basing his responses on (at least part of) what he reads is to make some hierarchical arrangement of the block's information.

An Einstellung hypothesis of primacy. It is of interest that the trend of results with reference to primacy effects followed a pattern similar to that found in experimental variations conducted to minimize Einstellung effects in problem-solving situations. This finding suggests that it may be possible to draw valid generalizations for a wide range of behavior concerning the factors and conditions which tend to minimize the influence of set.

Various other experimental findings also highlight the similarity between primacy effects and Einstellung effects in these problems. For example, it has been found that volume-measuring problems not solvable by the oft-repeated method (called extinction problems) tended to weaken the Einstellung. The second block of information might be regarded as an extinction block, since the actions described therein did not conform to the behavioral pattern implied in the first block. That the second block did tend to weaken the directional tendency fostered by the first block might be inferred from the fact that when the usual procedure was employed, E responses were less frequent after the EI communication

than after the E communication alone, and that I responses
were less frequent after the IE sequence than after the I
block.

Einstellung effects often were not found when the unitary
sequence of the set-inducing series was broken by intermin-
gling set-inducing problems with other kinds of problems.
Similarly, exploratory studies have shown that when the
sentences in the combined description were scrambled, thus
alternating sentences from the two blocks, primacy effects
were lower than when the usual order prevailed.

Retesting after a lapse of several hours or several days
revealed that Einstellung effects in the volume-measuring
problems tended to persist. Likewise, exploratory studies
have found primacy effects shortly after, one day after, and
one month after the original communication was given, even
though it was not reread during the interval.

Research has been initiated to maximize primacy effects by
introducing factors which tended to strengthen Einstellung
in the volume-measuring problems. Very pronounced Einstellung effects have been found under speed conditions; only
one preliminary study relating primacy to speed has been
completed to date, but it did show higher primacy effects
under speed conditions (when subjects were timed and told
to hurry) than under non-speed conditions.

These experimental findings lend support to the hypothesis that primacy is in the nature of an Einstellung.
Whether or not this hypothesis is accepted, systematic research can be undertaken to study what happens to primacy-
recency when conditions are varied, as they were in the investigations of Einstellung effects. Such a "variational approach" seems to be of value, both because it may reveal
the influence of various situational factors on the relative

strength of primacy or recency, and because it helps to explore the realm of applicability of tentative generalizations drawn from the model of the volume-measuring series.

If the Einstellung hypothesis of primacy is accepted, we still do not have an answer to the question of why primacy effects prevail under particular conditions or how they are brought about. After years of research with the volume-measuring problems, there are still many unanswered questions about the why and the how of Einstellung effects. Certain known results do suggest that overtly similar Einstellung effects may be brought about by different processes. Some individuals consciously generalized somewhere in the series that they were being given problems to which one method was applicable, while others seemed not to make such generalizations. Some were not aware that they were repeating one method while others were. Some made certain assumptions that favored the carry-over of the set method to the test problems, while others did not make these assumptions. Factors of learning, attention, and acceptance all seem to play roles in determining the strength of the Einstellung. Analogously, primacy effects may be brought about by different processes, in which factors of learning, attention, and acceptance may all be involved.

Order Effects within a Communication

CHAPTER 6

Need for Cognition and Order of Communication as Determinants of Opinion Change[1]

ARTHUR R. COHEN

THIS EXPERIMENT is an outgrowth of three general lines of research: (a) studies of the effects on opinion change of the manner in which arguments are organized (18); (b) studies of opinion change as determined by the relationship between needs of the individual and appeals of the communication (23, 24, 37, 40, 41); and (c) studies of the need for cognition (2, 6, 36, 39). It is concerned with whether information assumed to satisfy aroused needs will be accepted to a greater extent when it is presented before or after those needs have been aroused.

One set of conditions which might be expected to determine the relative effectiveness of different orders of argument concerns the position in which information is placed in relation to the arousal of needs which the information can

1. The author wishes to express his indebtedness to G. E. McDonnell for his invaluable aid in conducting and analyzing this experiment.

presumably satisfy. The major theoretical consideration raised by this problem centers around the issue of retroactive structuring in the interests of need satisfaction. It is assumed that information presented before a need-arousing talk has to be perceived as "apt" by the individual, as "fitting" the need arousal and as a possible way of resolving it. Information presented afterward can operate in a direct fashion for the individual; it may require less effort on his part for him to see it as tailored to the need-arousing situation.

This reasoning would seem to imply that information relevant to need satisfaction, when presented after strong needs have been aroused, will be more readily seen as satisfying those needs than information presented before need arousal. And, considering the research evidence relating need satisfaction to communication acceptance, we may expect the former situation to lead to greater acceptance of that information.

Previous research has suggested that people differ in their desire and ability to organize, understand, and make reasonable their experiential world. Such differences in motivation have been ascribed to differences among individuals in their need for cognition. The existence of differences in the strength of such a need to structure relevant situations in meaningful, integrated ways implies that persons will be differentially able to structure a communication situation retroactively in the interests of need satisfaction. Individuals with strong needs for cognition, in their efforts to maximize understanding, may be more willing or able to "fit" potentially need-satisfying information to a subsequent need arousal than those with weak needs for cognition. They may be better able to overcome the effects of reversal of a communication sequence more than persons with weak cognition needs. Thus need for cognition is seen as a significant factor in the interaction between order and the alleviation of emotional tension as they determine the acceptance of new information.

These considerations generate the following hypotheses: a communication situation in which information assumed to satisfy aroused needs is placed after need arousal will bring more acceptance of that information than a situation in which the information is placed before need arousal. Furthermore, in the face of the demand for retroactive structuring, individual differences in the strength of need for cognition will be a significant mediating factor in the effect of communication order.

Method

General design. An expanded "before-after" design was employed. The "before" measures comprised a device used to assess strength of need for cognition and an opinion questionnaire. Approximately one month later the subjects were given a talk on "problems of course grades." In this talk half of the subjects received a need-arousing talk followed by relevant information and half received relevant information followed by need arousal. This was immediately followed by an opinion questionnaire and a questionnaire designed to tap various reactions to the experimental situation as well as the amount of information retained. Three months later all subjects received another opinion questionnaire and an information test.

Subjects. Thirty-five students from a course in introductory psychology at Yale University make up the sample employed in the present experiment. They were divided into two groups, one of 18, the other of 17, and were seen at different times in their classroom during regularly scheduled class periods.

General experimental setting. For several weeks prior to the experiment the issues of grading and grading reforms were heightened on the Yale campus. Several articles had appeared in the campus newspaper carrying accounts of the "abundance of high grades" at Yale, the attitudes of administration and faculty toward the problem, and the possibilities of new and tougher grading systems. It was felt that this situation provided good material for the present investigation. The assumption of uniformly high motivation among the subjects may be made here; specific data on the uniformly great concern of the subjects over the grading system will be presented later.

"Before" measures. During a class meeting the total population of 35 subjects filled out a large opinion questionnaire on a number of different issues assumed to be important to them. Imbedded in this questionnaire was an item concerning their attitudes toward grading "on the curve" (i.e. according to relative standing in class). The questionnaire was made up of a series of a priori scales arranged as a "pick two" device; from 6 choice points, a 10-point scale could be generated. The subjects could be ordered according to the degree to which they agreed or disagreed that grading on the curve "would be a decided advantage." This issue provided the core for the information presented later in association with the need-arousing communication.

The subjects then completed a questionnaire designed to measure strength of need for cognition. This procedure has been used and reported elsewhere (6). Briefly, it consists of a group of forced choice reactions to a wide variety of hypo-thetical situations. One of three possible responses to each situation is assumed to indicate a desire for more information and/or understanding. In each situation the cognition state-ment is pitted against statements representing other needs; across all situations it is placed in juxtaposition to a number of different needs. On the basis of this measure the subjects were divided according to the strength of their need for cog-nition.

Experimental communication. Approximately one month later the subjects were divided into two groups, one of 17 and the other of 18, each group attending different discus-sion sessions. Both groups were introduced to a communi-cator who was supposedly a psychology department faculty member present to discuss current grading problems. This "faculty member" was said to be the chairman of a depart-ment committee concerned with evaluating grading prob-lems. He was said to be present in order to familiarize some of the students with these problems and to obtain the stu-dents' views of the issue and its probable outcome.

The *need-arousal* delivered by the communicator dealt with the entire grading problem. It was, in effect, a fear-arousing situation guaranteed to present the subjects with a bewildering array of vague and threatening possibilities. First, some accurate statistics on the rise of grades were given, followed by a series of speculations concerning quality of in-struction, academic acceptability, undoubted eventual low-ering of grades, negative reactions on the part of parents, professional schools and potential employers, and so forth. This was concluded with a vague statement to the effect that the entire situation had provoked a good deal of confusion, uncertainty, and resentment, and that there would probably be some penalties for all students concerned.

The information given in association with the need arousal centered around grading "on the curve." It presented this method of grading as an efficient, clear-cut system which would discriminate better among the students and resolve some of the difficulties in the present system. Further facts concerning the specific characteristics and operation of grading on the curve were given. This section was concluded with the statement that curve grading provided a system wherein "academic standards are maintained, the discriminatory ability of the faculty is maximized, and the individual student is given a great deal of consideration." Thus the information could be perceived as a way of satisfying the needs aroused in the other section: "grading on the curve" could be viewed as a judicious solution to the grading problem. The curve grading procedure was not advocated strongly or directly by the communicator, in order to allow differential perception by the subjects of its value in reducing the aroused tension. This procedure also permitted greater leeway in studying the effects of need for cognition on the degree to which the subjects made active efforts themselves to structure the information as relevant to the need-arousing communication. Finally, it minimized the perception of the information as persuasion or instruction (18).

In the *Ordered* condition (N = 17) the need arousal was presented first, followed by the information. In the *Reverse* condition (N = 18) the information was given first followed by the need arousal. This was the only difference between the two experimental conditions; both received exactly the same material.

"Immediate-after" measures. Following the communicator's

talk, the subjects were asked for their reactions, presumably in order to help the authorities evaluate the problem better and understand it more completely. The subjects first received an opinion questionnaire with the item concerning grading on the curve identical to the one presented at the pre-session one month earlier. After this, a number of measures were obtained. Most of these measures were taken on eight-point a priori scales. Measures of cognitive differentiation, complexity, and rational and informational characteristics of the cognitive field were adapted from a procedure developed by Zajonc (43) for describing cognitive structure. The measure required the subjects to list as many aspects of the present problem area as they could, i.e. all the qualities, characteristics, attributes and dimensions of the issue. This was followed by a sorting procedure which made it possible to derive measures of the extent to which the subject's cognitive field was elaborated and differentiated with regard to this issue. In addition, the characteristics listed were coded with reference to their rationality or nonemotionality.

The measures taken were the following:

1. *Frustration measures:*
   a. An index of degree of interest and liking for the presentation.
   b. Desires for additional material and information.
2. *Judgmental measures (judgment of the communicator):*
   a. Perception of the communicator in positive or negative terms. This takes into account his interest in a proper solution to the problem, his concern, his intelligence, his warmth or coldness and his personality organization.

    b. Accuracy of information: the degree to which the information presented by the communicator was true and accurate.

    c. Important facts: the degree to which the communicator took into account all the important facts.

3. *Cognition measures:*

    a. Closure satisfaction: the degree to which the issue seems possible of resolution and satisfaction with its resolution.

    b. Perception of the reasonableness of the communicator: the rationale for his position and presence.

    c. Number of characteristics in the cognitive field which are rationally, i.e. unemotionally toned.

4. *Information measures:*

    a. Cognitive differentiation with regard to the issue: a measure of the degree to which a cognitive set is elaborated, of the degree to which different aspects of a cognitive object are recognized and identified. Differentiation is designed to reflect amount of information, knowledge of the cognitive object and amount of experience with it.

    b. Cognitive complexity with regard to the issue: a measure of the extent of division and subdivision of the whole. The more divisions in a cognitive set, the more the parts thus isolated are themselves divided, the higher the degree of complexity of the field.

    c. An information test, directly gathering the subjects' information about the entire body of material presented.

Three months later, a final opinion questionnaire concerning grading "on the curve" was given which was identical with the two previous ones. The information test was also administered at this time.

Results

Effects of the experimental conditions on opinions. Table 11 presents the effects of the experimental conditions on opinion change and acceptance. There were no reliable differences among the groups in "before" opinions on the issue in question ($p = .39$). Since 5 represents the midpoint, it can be seen that both groups were somewhat on the negative side of the attitude dimension.

TABLE 11. *Mean Opinions on Issue at "Before," "Immediate-after," and "Delayed-after" for Each Experimental Group*

	Ordered ($N = 17$)	Reverse ($N = 18$)
Before	4.47	3.72
Immediate-after	6.29	3.33
Delayed-after	5.90	3.67

The results show that differences in the order of presenting information relative to the need-arousing communication have a significant effect on opinion acceptance. The group which received the need-arousal first and the information about curve grading second shows a more positive attitude toward the proposal than the group which received the reverse order. While there were no differences between the groups before the experimental communications, they are significantly different in their opinion immediately afterward, as well as three months afterwards. Covariance analyses were performed on the "immediate-after" scores and on the "delayed-after" scores, controlling on opinion scores on the "before" questionnaire. The difference at "immediate-after" is significant beyond the .01 level (F = 11.62), while that at "delayed-after" is significant beyond the .001 level (F = 16.99).[2]

Thus it appears that the position of the information in relation to the need-arousal had considerable effect on its acceptance, presumably because of the greater perception of its instrumental value in satisfying those needs.

Correlates of opinion acceptance. In view of the differential effect of the order of communication on opinions, it becomes important to see whether these differences are accompanied by differences in judgment of the communicator, or in frustration, cognition, or information in regard to the general issue. This allows a specification of some of the direct correlates of opinion change in this context and provides some further orientation toward the effects of the different experimental conditions. The data are in Table 12.

The data indicate that consistent with differences between the experimental groups in opinion change are differences between them with regard to how reasonable, organized, and rational they perceived the communicator and communication situations to be. No reliable differences between the groups appear with regard to judgmental, frustration, anxiety-related, or informational measures. It would seem that the opinion results are not associated with gross differences on these latter dimensions. Rather, they appear to be associated with an evaluation of the situation in terms of cognitive clarity and understanding. The individuals exposed to the reverse order perceived less possibility for closure and were less satisfied with the closure given; they felt the communicator and communication to be less reasonable and were less

2. All statistical tests in this chapter are two-tailed tests.

struck with the rationale offered; and they perceived the entire issue in less rational, less objective terms.

The relationship between the various opinion-related measures and opinion-change scores from "before" to "immediate-

TABLE 12. *Ordered Condition vs. Reverse Condition on Various Opinion-Related Measures*

	Ordered	Reverse	t	p-value
1. Frustration measures:				
a. Degree of Interest-like	12.73	12.55	.51	ns
b. Desires for more information	14.05	12.72	.98	ns
2. Judgmental measures:				
a. Perception of the communicator (positive-negative)	26.23	25.22	.68	ns
b. Accuracy of information:				
N judging accurate:	9	12	$x^2 = .69$	ns
N judging inaccurate:	8	6		
c. Important facts taken into account:				
N saying Yes:	11	9	$x^2 = .78$	ns
N saying No:	6	9		
3. Cognition measures:				
a. Closure-satisfaction	10.41	7.94	2.96	.01
b. Perception of reasonableness of communicator	17.29	14.72	1.94	.07
c. % of cognitive characteristics rational, nonemotional	.82	.62	2.43	.02
4. Information measures:				
a. Cognitive complexity	16.57	15.12	.72	ns
b. Cognitive differentiation	8.76	8.50	.31	ns
c. Information test	5.41	5.56	.11	ns

after" was also examined for the entire range of subjects. The data here show that the only significant correlations are those obtaining between closure-satisfaction and opinion change ($r = .46$, $p < .01$) and between perception of the communicator's reasonableness and opinion change ($r = .35$, $p < .05$). These results reflect the differences between the two experimental groups on opinion acceptance and on the cognition measures.

Need for cognition and communication order as they affect opinion change. The results in the preceding section would seem to indicate that perceptions related to cognitive clarity, meaning, order, and the like are associated with opinion change. They provide strong evidence for an evaluation of the condition requiring retroactive structuring as one containing strong elements of ambiguity, and for evaluation of the ordered condition as relatively well structured. Since the need for cognition was postulated as a major determinant of ability and desire for retroactive structuring, exploration of the effects of this need becomes an important next step.

Before examining the effects of need for cognition, it should be mentioned that no differences existed between the ordered and reverse conditions with regard to strength of this need. The means are 3.29 and 3.39. This permitted the distinction of four groups in the analysis of the effects of this need: Ordered-High Need for Cognition (N = 7), Ordered-Low Need for Cognition (N = 10), Reverse-High Need for Cognition (N = 9), the Reverse-Low Need for Cognition (N = 9).

The motivational question should be discussed first. It has been assumed that all subjects were greatly involved in the present issue; differences in interest and importance of the situation might have led to serious variations in attention. The validity of the assumption of high motivation may be supported by the following evidence. When asked about the disturbance students might feel over statements made in the need-arousing communication, i.e. the prospect of lowered grades, all subjects felt that their peers would be highly disturbed and felt this to an equal degree. On an eight-point scale with 1 indicating maximum disturbance, the means were: 2.33, 2.29, 2.00, and 2.10.

Table 13 presents the mean ratings on the opinion measure for each subgroup at the three times of measurement. The first thing to be noted is the difference between the high and low cognition subjects in their attitudes toward the issue on the "before" measure (t = 2.23, p = .05). Secondly, the opinion trends for each of the four experimental subgroups are strikingly different. Covariance analysis was performed on "delayed-after" scores, controlling on "before" scores. The F equals 9.83, p < .01.

If one concentrates on the differences between the high- and low-need groups at the "delayed-after" measurement it is quite evident that while the experimental conditions had a great influence on the lows, they made no difference for the highs. The covariance analysis shows that in addition to being exactly alike "before," both high-need cognition

TABLE 13. *Mean Opinions on Issue at "Before," "Immediate-after," and "Delayed-after" for Each Experimental Subgroup*

		STRENGTH OF NEED FOR COGNITION	
	Condition	High	Low
A. Before	Reverse	3.11	4.33
	Ordered	3.14	5.40
B. Immediate-after	Reverse	4.22	2.56
	Ordered	6.00	6.50
C. Delayed-after	Reverse	4.67	2.67
	Ordered	4.29	7.00

groups are alike at "delayed-after." However, while both low-need cognition groups were not significantly different "before," at "delayed-after" the ordered-low group is significantly

more positive toward the issue than the reverse-low group
($F = 21.34$, $p < .001$). The same is true at "immediate-after"
($F = 9.02$, $p < .01$).

As a group, the high cognition subjects show a significant
rise from "before" to "delayed-after" in spite of their differential exposure to the communications ($t = 2.23$, $p < .05$).
The ordered-low group shows no significant increase, while
the reverse-lows decrease ($t = 1.80$, $p < .10$). Furthermore,
the ordered-high group increases significantly in positive attitude from "before" to "immediate-after" ($t = 2.50$, $p < .02$)
and shows a significant decrease from "immediate-after" to
"delayed-after" ($t = 2.09$, $p < .05$). The reverse-highs, on the
other hand, show a small but steady rise from "before" to
"immediate-after" to "delayed-after." The ordered-high
group appears to have been initially affected to a great degree, though the effect is not lasting.

These results clearly indicate that while individuals can
be differentially affected by the order of a communication
situation (presumably as a function of degree of structuring
in the interests of need satisfaction) these effects may be confined to those persons with relatively weak cognitive needs.[3]

One last finding should be mentioned. When the change
in attitude toward the issue is examined from "immediate-
after" to "delayed-after," there appears to be a negative correlation between this change and perception of the communicator's qualities. It seems that the more favorably the communicator was regarded at the time of the "immediate-after"
measure, the more the loss in opinion acceptance from "im-

3. The question may be raised as to the relationship between cognitive
need and general intelligence. No direct evidence is yet available, but in the
present study the correlation between college grades and need for cognition
while positive is not significant ($r = + .23$). In previous research (6) need for
cognition was found to be uncorrelated with need for achievement.

mediate-after" to "delayed-after." The more unfavorably he is perceived at first, the more gain in opinion acceptance later ($r = -.39$, $p < .05$). This finding appears to parallel the well-known "sleeper effect" (19, 21).

Discussion

The assumption has been made in this chapter that when information on an advocated opinion is instrumental to need satisfaction, it will be accepted. In the present experiment it was further assumed that a situation in which information relevant to need satisfaction is given after the needs are aroused will be more easily structured in the interests of need satisfaction than a situation in which relevant information is placed before need-arousal. The latter instance was said to be one which demanded retroactive structuring, the former, direct structuring. Thus the ordered condition was expected to produce, and did produce, more opinion change than the reverse (retroactive) condition.

The demand for retroactive structuring in a communication situation seems to carry along with it a perception of relatively high ambiguity. The ordered and reverse groups were no different from one another on a host of frustration and informational measures. They did differ from one another, however, in the cognitive clarity and reasonableness which the subjects perceived as characteristic of the communication situation. These differences were consistent with differences in opinion on the issue considered. Thus differences between experimental groups in the effect of a communication on opinions need not be due to correlated differences in the learning and retention of the content of the communication. In the present situation they seem to be due to differences in perception of the situation as cognitively clear and reasonable.

Need satisfaction and presumably, therefore, opinion change in this situation demand the perception of the information as instrumental to the aroused need. The reverse condition may be more unclear than the ordered condition because it may be more difficult to perceive the information as apposite to a need-arousing communication. The ordered condition is fairly regular and expected and is part of the standard logical formulae of which we are all aware. That is, solutions generally follow exposure to a problem and to the questions raised; there are clear-cut guidelines and cues for behavior in the interests of need satisfaction. The reverse situation has fewer learned guidelines and cues for such behavior in the interests of need satisfaction; retroactive structuring is less common and less practiced. These differences in ease of behavior toward need satisfaction may in fact cover the differences between what are generally termed ambiguous and structured situations.

The interaction between need cognition and the experimental conditions was found to be extremely important for opinion change. The major finding in this regard concerns the differential effects of the experimental conditions on persons of high and low cognitive needs. While the different conditions make no difference for individuals with high cognitive needs over a three-month period, they are of considerable importance for the lows. The lows show a significant decrease in positive attitude toward the issue as a result of the reverse situation, thereby producing the striking differences at "delayed-after."

When the order is clear and presents meaningful cues and guidelines, the lows increase slightly in positive attitude;

when this situation is reversed, their weaker needs for cognitive clarity prevent them from making the considerable effort required to see the information as apt for the need arousal. They are more dependent upon the order presented by the communicator; they tend to accept the information when it is presented in order and do not apparently have high enough standards for cognitive clarity to screen it carefully over time. When presented with the reverse order, they may be frustrated by the ambiguity in the retroactive process and may be left with a negative, hostile, and rejecting attitude as a result of the fear and threat inherent in the need arousal which remains unresolved.

Individuals with strong cognitive needs, on the other hand, are less dependent upon the order presented by the communicator. There are no reliable differences among the highs between ordered and reverse conditions on either "immediate-after" or "delayed-after" measures. They seem to be no different over time regardless of the communication situation to which they are exposed. Apparently the high-cognition people, who make more of an effort toward cognitive clarity in general, are able to do so sufficiently well in the reverse condition to reach the level of their peers in the ordered condition.

Over time, however, both high-need groups show a slow but significant rise in positive attitude. It may be that the mere fact of information presented works on them over time, leading to a more positive evaluation of the issue than they had on the "before" measure. Interestingly enough, the highs who receive the ordered communication show a very strong initial effect immediately after receiving the communication. This is presumably related to the reinforcement inherent in satisfaction of their strong needs for understanding; receiving a clearly ordered communication makes this possible, and upon receiving it they fully accept the information supplied. However, over a three-month period their high standards for cognitive clarity appear to be asserted and they drop to the same point as the highs who received the reverse order, a point to which evaluation of new information per se may have brought all highs. It would also seem that these same high standards for cognitive clarity assumed to be part of the equipment of the highs are also responsible for their initially more negative attitude toward the issue than the lows on the "before" opinion measure. They may have more rigorous criteria for acceptable information and belief than the lows.

In reviewing the preceding argument, it may be said:

1. The highs who receive the ordered condition apparently accept the information initially because of a pervasive need to structure, and a clear communication which permits this. However, over time, their high standards for cognitive clarity may cause them to screen the information, thereby producing a sharp decrease in positive opinion.

2. The lows in the ordered condition receive the information in the maximally effective order but may not be motivated to screen it carefully over time. They thus remain highly positive.

3. The highs who receive the reverse condition are motivated to structure the situation retroactively. They show an opinion level over time equal to the other high group, a level they may have reached simply as a result of new information.

4. The lows in the reverse condition, by contrast with their "before" opinions, reject the information. This is probably related to unresolved residues of fear and anxiety due to their inability to structure the situation to the point where

the information is seen as relevant to satisfaction of the needs aroused in the communication.

Thus while it may be said with some degree of confidence that differential order affects opinion change, presumably because need satisfaction is differentially facilitated, this effect may over time be confined to those people with weak cognition needs who are more dependent upon the way material is presented and who are less motivated to structure material retroactively in the interests of need satisfaction.

One other factor appears to have been important for the effect of the communication over time. This concerns the perception of the communicator in a favorable or unfavorable light. It would seem that those with relatively negative attitudes toward him at the "immediate-after" measurement became slightly more positive about the issue over the period from "immediate-after" to "delayed-after" measurement; whereas those who were relatively more favorably disposed toward him became somewhat more negative about the issue. The similarity of this finding to that of the sleeper effect suggests that here, too, there has been some dissociation of content from source (the communicator). In this instance, the fact that the communication contained arguments and information which could be evaluated on their own merits without necessarily bringing the communicator to mind may have facilitated this process. Thus though there appears to have been a somewhat reduced effect of perception of the communicator immediately after the communications were given, over time such perceptions may become a meaningful factor in communication acceptance. Unfortunately the small N prevented exploration of the relationship of this judgmental index to the interaction between order and need cognition, as all three serve to determine opinion acceptance.

CHAPTER 7

Order of Presentation as a Factor in "Conditioning" Persuasiveness [1]

WILLIAM J. MCGUIRE

IT IS POSSIBLE to apply a learning theory analysis of the persuasion process to predict the effect upon persuasion of varying the order in which material is presented within a communication. If, for example, the source remains the same for a series of messages, the receipt of each message can be considered a separate conditioning trial on which the source constitutes a stimulus to which the response of agreement is being conditioned (or extinguished). In making this prediction it must be pointed out that the response of agreeing with the position advocated by the source comes only as the final response in a chain of stimulus-producing responses set off by the message. To be influenced, the recipient must make the preliminary responses of paying attention to the message, comprehending its contents, accepting the conclusions advo-

1. The study reported here was carried out when the author was a Social Science Research Council postdoctoral fellow at the Laboratory for Research in Social Relations at the University of Minnesota. The author is indebted to Leon Festinger and John Darley for their help in the implementation of the experiment.

cated, and rehearsing this acceptance sufficiently to permit later expression of the induced change on an attitude questionnaire. Should any of these intervening responses not be elicited, opinion change, the ultimate response whose evocation is sought, will not occur.

Under the conditions described, a conditioning trial occurs when the recipient's agreement response is evoked (through the mediation of the responses of attention, comprehension, etc.) and this agreement is reinforced. If the agreement response is evoked but not rewarded, an "extinction trial" occurs. Hence earlier messages from a source may augment or reduce the recipient's agreement with later ones, depending upon whether his agreement with the earlier messages was rewarded or not. Furthermore, if agreement with the earlier messages was actually punished, their receipt may have constituted "avoidance training." In this case the recipient's tendency to agree with later messages will be even weaker than if agreement with the earlier messages was simply not rewarded. These predictions can be derived from the postulates of Hull's (22) learning theory.

In the study reported in this chapter, the conditions required for testing the above predictions were achieved by having a single source transmit a series of messages each arguing for the likelihood of occurrence of some future contingency. Some of the contingencies were pleasant, and therefore agreeing that their occurrence was likely would be rewarding, while others were undesirable, and hence agreement with their likelihood was apt to be punishing. It was predicted that when those messages supporting the likelihood of pleasant contingencies were presented first and those supporting the likelihood of unpleasant contingencies offered later, a greater total amount of agreement with the message contents would be evoked than when the messages were presented in reverse order, i.e. with the undesirable messages followed by the desirable ones.

It was further hypothesized that this effect of sequence on opinion change would be mediated by the effect of the earlier messages on the intervening responses of attending to and comprehending the message contents. The responses of paying attention to and comprehending the earlier messages would have led to greater learning and therefore acceptance of the positions advocated. Provided the earlier messages argued for the future occurrence of a desirable event, this acceptance response would be rewarded for the recipient. When, on the other hand, the earlier messages were undesirable ones, acceptance of their position would be unrewarding or even punishing. Receipt of these earlier unpleasant messages would then serve as avoidance training trials in which the recipient would learn to withhold attention and comprehension, with the result that later messages from this same source, even though they argued for pleasant positions, would effect less persuasion, since their pleasant contents would not be so readily recognized and learned by the recipient.

Methodology

Materials. An attitude questionnaire was administered to the subjects one week before a set of persuasive communications, again immediately after, and once again one week following these communications. The precommunication questionnaire contained 34 statements regarding events concerning college life (e.g. federal aid to permit free issuance of textbooks to college students; the increased scheduling of 7 A.M. classes to ease the classroom shortage). Beneath each statement was a scale for rating the likelihood of the event's occurrence. This scale consisted of a five-inch horizontal line marked off by short vertical lines every half an inch. These vertical lines were labeled, successively from left to right, by the numbers 0, 10, 20, . . . 90, 100. To the left of the scale was written "Very Improbable End" and to the right, "Very Probable End." The subjects received instructions telling them to draw a line through the scale at the point indicating their guess as to the likelihood of occurrence of the event in question. The scale was explained in terms of betting odds, with illustrative examples. Questions raised by the subjects regarding this concept were answered by the experimenter. All of the communications described below presented arguments designed to increase these "likelihood" ratings.

In another part of the same questionnaire all 34 statements were repeated together with a different type of scale, consisting of five boxes labeled, from left to right, "Very Much in Favor," "Somewhat in Favor," "Don't Care," "Somewhat Against," "Very Much Against." This time the subjects were instructed to indicate, not whether they thought the statement to be true, but whether they would like it to be true—that is, to indicate by marking an "X" in the appropriate box their impression of the desirability of the situation described. (These "desirability" ratings were used only to provide an objective basis on which to manipulate the independent variable—the order of the messages with respect to their "desirability," i.e. the subjects' drive or wise to agree with them.)

On the basis of their desirability scores on the first administration of the questionnaire, eight statements were selected to serve as critical issues on which persuasive communications were to be given. These statements were selected so that four were highly desirable items, i.e. items that the subject wished very much to be true (e.g. increased federal aid would permit free issuance of textbooks to college students). The other four were low desirability items, i.e. items that the subject wished very much not to be true (e.g. more classes would be scheduled at 7 A.M. to relieve the classroom shortage).

One week after this questionnaire the persuasive communications were presented to the subjects. Each communication consisted of the reply of a (fictitious) "Dr. Harold Wilson" to a question asked him during a press conference purportedly held on the occasion of his election to the presidency of the "National Association of University Administrators." Each communication consisted of a sheet of paper on which was mimeographed an interviewer's question and Dr. Wilson's 150-to-200-word reply. The question to which Dr. Wilson's comment served as answer for any one of the eight messages was actually one of the eight critical items contained in the questionnaire. Each of Dr. Wilson's eight replies consisted of a plausible, factual argument maintaining that the event in question was, in fact, likely to occur.

After the communications had been read by the subjects, the second questionnaire was administered. This questionnaire was identical with the one given a week earlier and described above, except for a new cover sheet and one additional page at the beginning. This added page contained a seven-item multiple-choice test of comprehension and memory for the contents of the communications. An item was also included asking the subject for his evaluation of Dr. Wilson's fairness to be indicated by one of the following choices: "completely fair," "almost completely fair," "mostly fair, though unfair in a few places," or "unfair in many places." (Since each subject, as explained below, received only four of the eight messages, there were two forms of this multiple choice test, each subject receiving the questions referring to the four messages which had been communicated to him.)

A week after the second administration, without any additional experimental communication, the questionnaire was administered for the third time. This final form was similar to that used in the first administration, without the extra pages of questions on content and fairness.

Procedure. The study involved three experimental sessions of 50 minutes each. The first was devoted to the precommunication administration of the questionnaire (which was represented to the subjects as part of a study to determine students' views on various matters pertaining to university planning).

The second session took place one week later and was devoted to giving the communications and the second administration of the questionnaire. The purpose of this session was represented to the subjects as an attempt to measure the comprehensibility of information on controversial topics obtained during an unrehearsed interview situation such as is found in court rooms, press conferences, congressional hearings, etc. The communications were presented in mimeographed form, one question and reply to the page. Two minutes were allowed for the reading of each page, in the prescribed order. Subjects were instructed to turn to the next page only when so directed and not to turn back to earlier pages at any time (this procedure being followed to control the order in which the communications were received).

The third session occurred one week later and was devoted to the third administration of the questionnaire and to explaining to the subjects the actual purpose of the experiment, pointing out to them the various deceits employed and the reasons for their employment.

Design. In order to set up efficiently a no-communication

control condition, an experimental design was used in which each subject received only four of the eight communications, two supporting highly desirable points of view and the other two supporting low desirability positions. The crucial independent variable was the order in which the four communications were presented: half of the subjects received the two high desirability communications first and then the two low desirability ones (the *H–L* group); the other half received the low desirability communications first, then the highly desirable ones (the *L–H* group).

Subjects. The data reported for the first and second administrations of the questionnaire are based on 92 subjects who were present for both sessions. Forty-six served in the *H–L* condition and 46 in the *L–H*. The data for the third administration are based on only 85 subjects, since 7 of the original subjects were absent on that day. All subjects were enrolled in a course in the general college of a large state university.

Results

As explained above, all of the subjects rated, on each administration of the questionnaire, the subjective probability of occurrence of eight different events. Four communications were given to each subject and were followed immediately by the second administration of the questionnaire. With each of the eight items, half of the 92 subjects served as a "control," receiving no communication on that item; the other 46 subjects received a communication arguing in favor of the likelihood of occurrence of the event described in the item. Of these 46 subjects who received communications on that item, 23 were in an H–L group (i.e. received the high desirability messages first, followed by the low desirability ones) and the other 23 were in an L–H group. (Each of the 92 subjects served as control on four of the items and received communications on the other four.)

Results on the main hypothesis regarding the effect of order on opinion change. It was predicted that the persuasive effect of the communication on any item would tend to be higher under the H–L condition than the L–H. This prediction is given substantial support by the results shown in Table 14. The simplest test of the hypothesis is provided by

TABLE 14. *Mean Ratings of the Probability of Occurrence of Eight Events Made before and after Receipt of Communications Arguing in Favor of Their Probability of Occurrence.*

		ITEMS								
ADMINISTRATION	CONDITION	1	2	3	4	5	6	7	8	MEAN
First (one	H-L	63	57	60	50	54	57	42	71	57
week before	L-H	59	43	61	48	55	68	41	82	57
communication)	Control	64	45	60	40	48	62	46	82	56
Second (immed-	H-L	77	76	72	62	78	82	68	80	74
iately after	L-H	70	70	68	56	75	84	62	79	70
communication)	Control	60	44	58	50	57	62	46	79	57
Third (one	H-L	67	68	62	67	64	76	54	77	67
week after	L-H	61	59	59	54	66	82	46	81	64
communication)	Control	64	49	58	50	59	55	40	76	55

considering just two of the rows in this table, namely the second administration rating of the eight items in the H–L row compared with those in the L–H, ignoring for the moment precommunication data. The results are in the predicted direction, i.e. the ratings are higher in the H–L condition than in the L-H for seven of the eight items. This result is significant at the .07 level on the basis of a sign test. (Throughout this chapter all significance levels are given on the basis of a "two-tail" test.)

A more sensitive test is possible by taking into account the size of these differences and analyzing the variance of the 16 scores into three components: H–L vs. L–H order (df = 1), items (df = 7), and interaction (df = 7), using the latter as the error term. The resulting F-ratio of order to error is significant at the .01 level.[2]

The above tests are based only on the postcommunication data. However, since a "before-after" design was used, recourse can be had also to corresponding precommunication scores. It can be seen by comparison of the precommunication scores for the H–L and L–H conditions that the higher postcommunication scores of the H–L condition cannot be accounted for by a sampling artifact. The over-all mean precommunication scores shown in Table 14 are practically identical for the two conditions, indicating that these groups were well equated initially.

A difficulty in the way of using the change scores between first and second administration of the questionnaire is the existence of a high correlation between precommunication scores and the amount of change. This suggests the operation of a ceiling effect. In this case the correlation between initial level and amount of gain (equal to postcommunication minus precommunication scores) is —.65 for the H–L condition and —.76 for the L–H condition. This artifact makes it unwise to test the hypothesis in terms of the simple gain scores. An appropriate statistical method for taking the correlated initial levels into consideration is a covariance analysis. In this way

2. There is some a priori basis for suspecting that some of the items are correlated, since the same group of subjects supplied data on blocks of four items within a condition (one block consisted of items 1, 2, 7, and 8, and the other of items 3, 4, 5, and 6). Hence, it might have been more appropriate to use only the within-blocks variance as the error term for the between-order effect. However, since the block effect is negligible, the between-block variance has been included in the error term.

the expected postcommunication levels for the two treatments could be estimated on the basis of the precommunication level and the correlation between the pre- and postcommunication levels. Any deviation of the obtained postcommunication treatment levels from the expected postcommunication levels could be attributed to the effect of the treatment. Following this procedure, the F-ratio between the adjusted mean square for order and the adjusted interaction (error) mean square is significant on the .001 level for 1 and 6 degrees of freedom. Hence, by any of the statistics reported the effect is in the predicted direction and of a magnitude that can be considered statistically significant.[3]

The scores from the third administration (as shown in the last three rows of Table 14) indicate that the effect of the communication has been partially dissipated after the passage of one week's time, which is consonant with the usual findings in such studies. However, both treatments still exceed the control group by highly significant amounts. The differential between the two communication conditions (H–L and L–H) has declined somewhat after one week but is still apparent.[4]

3. A second technique for compensating for ceiling effects is the use of the "efficiency index" proposed by Hovland, Lumsdaine, and Sheffield (19) for this purpose. The index is equal to $(P_2 - P_1) / (100 - P_1)$, where P_2 is the posttreatment percentage and P_1 the pretreatment percentage. Use of such a statistic in the present case supports the hypothesis, since by this index also the gain is greater in the H–L condition for seven of the eight items. By an analysis of variance on these scores (similar to that described above for the second administration scores), the superiority of the H–L treatment is significant on the .04 level.

4. The scores shown in the cells of Table 14, which have been the basis of the discussion until now, are the means of the individual subject's ratings of the "subjective probability of occurrence" of each of the eight events. There is some question whether it is valid to compute the mean of such "probability" scores by simply adding the individual ratings and dividing this sum by the number of scores, since this assumes an equal-unit scale. A plausible

Results bearing on the hypothesized mechanisms underlying this main effect. It was hypothesized that the order variable would have its effect on opinion change through the mediation of attention and comprehension responses: when the earlier messages supported desirable positions, any attention to and comprehension of them would result in more learning and therefore [5] more acceptance of their contents, which would constitute a rewarding state of affairs. Hence attention and comprehension of later messages would be enhanced. When, on the other hand, the earlier messages supported undesirable positions, any greater learning and therefore acceptance of their contents would constitute a punishing state of affairs, so that attention to, and comprehension

case can be made for considering these ratings as being based on a proportion or percentage scale. In this case it would be necessary to transform these individual percentages scores to an equal-interval scale by, e.g. the arcsine transformation, and to find the mean by summing these transformed scores and dividing by the N. Such a transformation should also reduce the troublesome "ceiling effects" discussed elsewhere. When the obtained individual scores from the present study are actually transformed by such an operation, the resulting means show the predicted effect for all eight items (rather than seven out of eight as with the nontransformed scores reported above) and by the various parametric tests reported above the effects are significant at still higher levels of confidence than are those calculated from the nontransformed scores as reported above. However, although the transformed scores support the hypotheses at higher levels of confidence, the results in Table 14 are given in terms of the nontransformed scores because these seemed simpler to interpret.

5. Implied in this statement is the assumption that there is a direct relationship between the extent of learning of a persuasive message and the amount of opinion change produced. This assumption, which is commonly made and is rather obvious in the extreme case of no learning, receives empirical support from the data collected in this study, which indicate a biserial correlation coefficient of .53 between learning and opinion change. This correlation coefficient is based on a dichotemization of the 92 subjects on the basis of learning scores into those who made zero errors on the multiple-choice test, a total of 37 subjects, and those who made one or more errors, a total of 55 subjects. The opinion change score was the total number of points by which the subject increased his probability ratings of the four events on which he received communications.

of, later messages would be avoided. Thus subjects in the H–L group should have shown better learning of the contents of the messages than subjects in the L-H groups. An opportunity to test this hypothesis was furnished by the results of the seven-item multiple-choice test on the content of the communications which each subject answered immediately after reading the set of messages. The results of this test lend considerable support to the operation of this hypothesized mechanism. Of the 46 subjects in the H–L group, 23 made perfect scores on this recall test, while of the 46 subjects in the L–H group only 14 received perfect scores, a difference in the predicted direction, statistically significant at the .06 level on the basis of a chi-square test. It appears then that the receipt of undesirable information in the source's earlier messages results in lessened learning by the recipient of later messages from that source and therefore in their lessened influence.

It is possible, on the basis of data collected in this experiment, to test two alternative hypotheses regarding the mechanism underlying the main effect of order of messages on opinion change. It might be hypothesized that the order variable had its effect on opinion change through its influence on source-credibility; specifically, in the H–L group, the pleasant contents of the earlier messages might have caused an up-rating in the recipient's impressions of source credibility, while in the L–H condition, the earlier (low desirability) messages might have resulted in down-rating the source's credibility position. If such change in source credibility did occur, it would account for the principal finding, since previous experimenters (21, 26) have found the amount of opinion change to be directly related to source credibility. Some data obtained in the present study can be brought to bear on this hypothetical mechanism. After receipt of the messages subjects were asked to state whether they thought the source, Dr. Wilson, had been "completely fair," "almost completely fair," "mostly fair though unfair in a few places," or "unfair in many places." The results lend little support to this hypothesized mechanism. Of the 46 subjects in the H–L condition, 26 rated the source as completely fair, and of the 46 subjects in the L–H condition, 24 rated him as completely fair, a difference in the expected direction but of quite negligible magnitude.[6]

A second alternative hypothesis regarding the underlying mechanism for the main effect is that the obtained relationship between order of messages and amount of opinion change is due to a habituation rather than a reinforcement phenomenon. This habituation hypothesis holds that the greater effectiveness of the H–L order derives from the fact that the recipient had more initial agreement with the desirable positions and hence is habituated to accept the source's later messages. According to stimulus-response reinforcement theory, however, the crucial aspect of the earlier messages in the present experimental situation is not the extent of the recipient's agreement with them, but rather the extent of his reward (or punishment) for agreeing with them, since initial agreement without reward would constitute an extinction trial rather than a habit-strengthening trial. The habituation hypothesis is based on the law of frequency postulated by contiguity theory, rather than the law of effect postulated by reinforcement theory.

6. Of course, the lack of support given by our data does not definitely rule out the possible importance of some source-credibility mechanism underlying the main effect, since the present test is based on a question that probably constitutes a rather crude measure of source credibility and that would more appropriately have been asked immediately after the first two messages rather than after all the messages had been communicated.

Aside from the question of its theoretical derivation, the empirical validity of the habituation hypothesis is called into question by the present data. As it happens, the undesirable contingencies (numbers 5, 6, 7, and 8 of Table 14) are actually given on the precommunication questionnaire a probability of occurrence rating slightly higher than the desirable ones; furthermore, the messages on these contingencies happen to be somewhat more effective in producing opinion change, although both differences are well within the chance range. Hence the H–L desirability order of messages actually constitutes to some extent a low-high initial agreement sequence, and the L–H desirability order, a high-low initial agreement sequence. The data, therefore, indicate that whatever habituation effect there might be from the extent to which the recipient *did* agree with the earlier messages is overridden by the extent to which he had *wished* to agree with those earlier messages. It appears, then, that the crucial ordering variable influencing opinion change is the extent to which the recipient likes to agree with the messages, and not the extent to which he actually does agree with them.

On the basis of these results regarding the various alternative mechanisms which might underly the main effect, it would seem that after receiving the earlier undesirable messages, the subject can be thought of as saying to himself, "What this man says appears to be true, but I find it unpleasant and so I am not going to listen to him any more." In this way he avoids receiving information from the source and hence escapes persuasion. The subject who, on the other hand, receives earlier desirable messages can be thought of as saying to himself, "This man's comments are pleasant and worth listening to and so I shall pay close attention to him." Thus he receives more of the source's later arguments and as a result is influenced by them. It appears that even within a presumably "captive" audience, the device of selective self-exposure to information can operate.

One assumption in the present study particularly needs further testing. It has been assumed that the obtained effect of sequence on acceptance was a double one: that when the earlier messages were undesirable, the later ones were less accepted, and when the earlier messages were desirable, the later ones were more accepted. However, it could be that the obtained effect was due to only one of these factors, e.g. that the earlier desirable messages had no impact on the acceptance of the later ones, and all the obtained effect was due to the earlier undesirable messages' negative impact. Further study to decide this point would employ a third group of subjects who receive first neutral messages, then the later desirable (or undesirable) ones.

Discussion

Two main findings emerge from the study reported in this chapter. First, it was shown that the effect of a source's earlier communications on the persuasiveness of his later messages depends in large measure on the extent to which agreement with those earlier communications was rewarding for the recipient. Second, it was demonstrated that the effectiveness of a persuasive communication depends not only on its capacity for evoking the agreement response *per se* but also on its capacity for evoking those other responses which must mediate between the presentation of the communication and the ultimate response of agreeing with its content, i.e. such responses as paying attention to the message, studying its contents, accepting its arguments, and rehearsing one's agreement with its conclusion.

These two findings in conjunction suggest some further hypotheses regarding the influence of the order variable (and of other variables as well) on the effectiveness of persuasive communications under conditions other than those which obtained in the present experiment. The prediction can be made, for example, that the effect of earlier communications on later ones will be influenced by the rewards involved in many other types of motivational states besides the one manipulated in the present study (namely desirability or undesirability of the specific positions taken within the communications). Other possible motivations would include those which influence the recipient's learning of a communication (such as tolerance for ambiguity, need for cognition, and perceptual defense) and also those which affect his acceptance of the position advocated (such as need for identifying with a high-prestige communicator, need to conform to the norms of one's reference groups, etc.).

Furthermore, the implication of the present study, that the ultimate response of agreeing with or rejecting the position advocated in the communication is evoked only through the mediation of a chain of stimulus-producing responses (such as attention, comprehension, etc.) suggests the kind of restriction which must be placed on any hypothesis concerning the effect of some variable (such as personality characteristics of the recipient or type of media used) on amount of opinion change produced. In predicting the effect of a recipient's personality characteristic, e.g. suspiciousness, on the ease of producing opinion change it is necessary to take into account separately the effect of this personality variable on each of the responses intervening between presentation of the message and ultimate agreement on the part of the recipient. A suspicious person might be more likely to comprehend the contents of a message—because of the closer scrutiny to which he subjects the world—but might be less likely to accept those arguments which he does comprehend. Hence he might be more or less persuasible than a less suspicious person depending on whether, in a given communication situation, the main obstacle to opinion change is comprehension of the arguments or their acceptance.

Somewhat analagously, predicting the relative effectiveness of various communication channels (e.g. face-to-face vs. mass media) requires separate consideration of the effects of these media on comprehension of material presented, and on acceptance of the material comprehended. Face-to-face communication, for example, might be more effective than mass media in producing message comprehension but less effective in producing acceptance. Hence, in order to specify which communication channel would be the more effective, it would be necessary to specify for the given situation whether the main obstacle to opinion change lay in comprehension or in acceptance, considering both types of recipients and of messages involved.

There is great promise that a substantially better understanding of the influence process can be obtained from an application of stimulus response reinforcement theory principles to the communication persuasion situation. However, the maximum realization of this promise awaits a fuller analysis and specification of the human motives and needs which determine the reinforcing qualities of a given communication situation, and a fuller analysis into stimulus and response terms, of the process intervening between the presentation of a message and the recipient's ultimate acceptance or rejection of its arguments.

CHAPTER 8

Effects of Alternative Ways of Ordering Pro and Con Arguments in Persuasive Communications

IRVING L. JANIS AND ROSALIND L. FEIERABEND

ACCORDING to recent experimental evidence, a communication which includes opposing arguments may, under certain conditions, be more successful in persuading the audience than one which presents only the positive arguments supporting the communicator's position. An experiment reported by Hovland, Lumsdaine, and Sheffield (19) showed that a two-sided version of a radio program was more effective than a one-sided version in convincing those members of the audience who were initially opposed to the communicator's position. In a similar study by Lumsdaine and Janis (33), a two-sided communication proved to be markedly more effective than a one-sided one when the audience was subsequently exposed to counterpropaganda. Since these experiments were concerned with the over-all effects of introducing the opposing arguments into persuasive communications, no attempt was made to investigate variations in the ordering of the arguments.

The present investigation is concerned with the effect of the timing or sequence in which pro and con arguments are introduced. The communication involves the use of a special type of two-sided message. It does not consist of arguments which are mutually contradictory, in the sense of their refuting each other on the same point. Rather, pro and con arguments are designed to bring to light separate and unrelated aspects of the issue; the pro arguments point to the necessity for adopting the communicator's conclusions while the con arguments indicate the disagreeable concomitants which form an inevitable and integral part of the proposed action.

Whenever con arguments are introduced into a persuasive communication, the communicator faces an important dilemma. On the one hand, he would like to gain the advantages of a two-sided presentation. For example, as in the experimental study referred to above (33), he may wish to have the audience decide upon a political issue when the negative arguments are in evidence, so as to inoculate them against subsequent counterpropaganda. Or he may wish to give forewarnings about the unfavorable consequences that could result from his action recommendations, so as to prevent unpleasant surprise, disillusionment, and subsequent defections. On the other hand, however, the communicator takes the risk of weakening the persuasive effect of his communication if he includes opposing arguments. He may even unintentionally sway the audience to the side of his opponents.

The present study, then, attempts to obtain further information about the conditions under which the introduction of the opposing arguments will minimize the risk of producing boomerang effects while gaining the advantages of a two-sided presentation. The specific problem is that of comparing the pro-first sequence of arguments with the con-first sequence in those two-sided communications which emanate from a high-prestige source. For such communications it is assumed that the favorable attitude of the recipients toward the source predisposes them to be relatively uncritical as to the truth value and cogency of the main arguments. For convenience such messages are referred to as "authoritative communications."

Our main hypothesis is that when the opposing arguments have a very *low* probability of being spontaneously salient for the audience, an authoritative communication will be more effective if the con arguments are presented *after,* rather than *before,* the major pro arguments. That is, con arguments are expected to create less interference with audience acceptance if given toward the end of an authoritative communication, rather than near the beginning.

This can be regarded as a "primacy" hypothesis, since it asserts that under the specified conditions, whichever arguments are presented *first* will exert a *greater* influence. If the pro arguments are given before the con, the probability of audience acceptance of the communicator's conclusions will be maximized; if the con arguments are given before the pro, the chances of audience rejection will be increased.

This hypothesis is specifically formulated, however, only for nonsalient con arguments, i.e. those which the recipients have not previously heard about or which they do not spontaneously recall during the communication. It is predicated on the assumption that the probability of attaining a successful outcome is significantly increased if negative (con) incentives are not made salient until after the full motivational impact of the positive (pro) incentives has been realized. This theoretical assumption and a number of related ones pertaining to the arrangement of arguments in two-sided communications are explicated in Appendix B, which presents a theoretical analysis of the effects of pro and con arguments in terms of approach and avoidance conflicts (cf. below, pp. 170–86). The main implications of the analysis are the following: If con arguments are made salient at the very beginning of the communication, the recipient's avoidance motivation becomes comparatively strong at the outset and thus there will be a high probability that the remainder of the communication will be critically disputed or ignored. When pro arguments and appeals are presented first, however, the audience's motivation to accept the communicator's conclusions will tend to increase, thereby permitting the negative incentives to be tolerated. Furthermore, when the pro-first order is used, the predominance of approach over avoidance motivation during the early part of the communication may facilitate the termination of incipient conflict by a clear-cut decision to accept the communicator's position. Once the recipient reaches a conflict-reducing decision to conform with the communicator's judgments, he is less likely to be unduly influenced by the subsequent con arguments. Thus, for the communication situation specified, the chances of successful persuasion should be increased if the communicator presents most or all of his strong pro arguments before introducing any nonsalient con arguments. The following experiment was designed to compare the effectiveness of the pro-first with the con-first order of arguments in an authoritative communication.

Methods and Procedures

The persuasive communication was a pamphlet urging high school students to volunteer in their local Civil Defense Organization. This communication was chosen because it meets the essential conditions of an authoritative communication which promotes a specific point of view and, at the same time, is representative of those messages for which a communicator would find it desirable to include the opposing arguments. The con arguments serve to familiarize the audience with those unpleasant aspects which they would soon discover for themselves if they actually did volunteer. In the absence of such information, many individuals might respond positively at first, only to become disillusioned, discouraged, or disgruntled upon discovering the unpleasant features of the activity. Thus we used a communication whose goal was not only to influence people in the direction of a recommended course of action but also to prevent subsequent backsliding.

One essential reason for selecting the topic was that the con arguments were not likely to be spontaneously salient for most high school subjects, especially since they generally regarded it as unpatriotic to hold an unfavorable attitude toward civil defense. This expectation was confirmed by preliminary questions given to a separate sample of students. In response to these questions, students showed mainly unstructured and positive stereotyped opinions concerning civil defense preparations rather than judgments based on familiarity with the major pros and cons of the issue.

Several features of the experimental situation were designed to impress the audience with the *authoritative* character of the communication. The printed communication carried a heading which informed the reader that it was a pamphlet prepared by a local educational committee helping to recruit volunteers for the national Civil Defense Organization. The tone of the pamphlet was similar to that of official government statements to the general public and the appeal for volunteers was made in the name of the United States government. Furthermore, the status of the source was augmented by the social context in which the communication was presented: the pamphlet was distributed in the classrooms of a public high school, with time taken out of the regular curriculum to enable the students to read it.

The communication began with an introduction which stated the government's need for civil defense volunteers. This was followed by fourteen paragraphs, each embodying a separate argument, and a fifteenth paragraph which was an explicit plea for volunteers. Among the fourteen arguments, seven were designed to be strongly pro and seven as mildly con. Pro arguments stressed that dangers could be averted and that many lives could be saved through adequate civil defense warning and rescue activities. Con arguments pointed to such undesirable aspects as the tedium and inconvenience of all-night plane-spotting vigils, and the lack of public recognition granted to civil defense workers. The same communication was prepared in two forms which differed only in the sequential arrangement of the arguments. In one form, the seven pro arguments were presented first and in the other form the seven con arguments came first. The heading, the introduction and the concluding statements were the same for both forms.

Subjects were 182 students in the sophomore and junior classes of a New Haven, Connecticut, high school. They were given the communication during a study period, in their usual class groups. Subjects were divided into two experimental groups (each of $N = 63$) and one control group ($N = 56$). Each experimental subject received one of the two forms of the communication, either pro arguments first or con arguments first, followed by a questionnaire designed to test his attitude with respect to volunteering for civil defense activity. The two alternative forms of the communication were interleaved for distribution so that the subjects were divided at random into the two experimental groups. The subjects in the control group, however, received only the questionnaire.

In order to check on the assumption that seven of the arguments were, in fact, perceived as pro and the other seven as con, a rating procedure was carried out with an additional group of 48 subjects in the same high school. For this purpose a special version of each form of the communication was prepared, containing a rating scale directly below the introduction and one below each paragraph. Each scale contained five categories, ranging from "Very Poor" through "Neutral" to "Very Good," and subjects were asked to give their ratings in response to the following question: "Is this paragraph good or poor from the standpoint of making you want to volunteer for civil Defense?"

Results

The validity of the experimenters' choice of the pro and con arguments was ascertained by the judgments of the supplementary group of 48 subjects who were drawn from the same high school population as the subjects in the experimental groups. A very high percentage of the subjects in this supplementary group gave ratings of "fairly good" or "very good" to each of the seven pro arguments. The con arguments, on the other hand, received a relatively low percentage of favorable ratings. Every one of the pro arguments received a significantly higher percentage of favorable ratings than any of the con arguments.

We turn now to the central question which the experiment

was designed to answer: What effect, if any, does the sequential order of pro and con arguments have on the audience's postcommunication attitudes?

TABLE 15. *Comparison of Experimental Groups on Attitude toward Civil Defense and Willingness to Volunteer Following Exposure to a Two-sided Persuasive Communication*

	GROUP A Pro Arguments First ($N = 63$)	GROUP B Con Arguments First ($N = 63$)	GROUP C Controls: No Communication ($N = 56$)
Attitude toward Civil Defense *			
Item 1. Rejects counter-propaganda urging a *small* number of Civil Defense volunteers.	84.0%	73.0%	69.6%
Willingness to volunteer **			
Item 2. Favorably disposed toward volunteering for Civil Defense.	11.1	3.2	5.4
Item 3. Willing to sign up for a full year of Civil Defense work.	9.5	3.2	7.2
Item 4. Planning to contact the local Civil Defense headquarters in order to volunteer.	6.4	4.8	7.2
Combined index: Favorable response on one or more of the four items:	87.3%	73.0%	69.6%

* For Item 1, the 14.4 per cent difference between Group A and the control group is reliable at the 5 per cent confidence level (one tail); the 11 per cent difference between Groups A and B approaches the same level of confidence ($p < .07$).

Resistance to counterpropaganda was determined in the following way: After having read the authoritative pamphlet which favored a large civil defense organization, subjects were asked to read three paragraphs from a different source which presented a conflicting point of view as to the present need for volunteers in Civil Defense. The counterpropaganda arguments maintained that despite the fact that some government leaders feel it is important to have large numbers of volunteers for Civil Defense, other eminent leaders advocate maintaining only a small number of volunteers at the present time, since we are not today in a state of emergency and hence need nothing more than a small skeleton staff.

Subjects were then asked the following question:

(Item 1): Which one of these two views do you agree with?

_____ Think there should *not* be large numbers of volunteers for Civil Defense at present.

_____ Undecided.

_____ Think there should be large numbers of volunteers at present.

** For Item 2, the differences are in the predicted direction, but cannot be regarded as highly reliable (p = .08 for Group A versus Group B). This item contributes very slightly to the group differences shown by the Combined Index. On the remaining two items, the group differences are negligible and thus contribute nothing to the results based on the combined index.

The three items were worded as follows:

Item 2. How do you personally feel about volunteering for Civil Defense activity?

_____ Definitely plan to volunteer

_____ Will consider volunteering

_____ Might possibly volunteer

_____ Probably will *not* volunteer

_____ Definitely will *not* volunteer

Item 3. Are you willing to join the New Haven Civil Defense Organization for a *full year* (to work 4 hours *every* week)?

_____ I do not wish to join

_____ I am not ready to join now but might later

_____ I am not ready to join now but definitely plan to join later

_____ I am willing to sign up right now for a year's work

Item 4. In order to volunteer for Civil Defense work, you must apply to the Civil Defense Office in New Haven. Are you planning to telephone or go to visit the New Haven Civil Defense Office, in order to volunteer?

_____ Yes

_____ Undecided

_____ No

The main results are shown in Table 15. The over-all index used for comparing the experimental groups is the percentage of subjects expressing a favorable response to one or more of the four key items concerning attitude toward civil defense participation. On this index, Group A, which received the pro arguments first, is clearly superior to Group B, which received the con arguments first (p-value = .05, one tail). Group A also differs significantly from the control group which had received no communication (p-value < .05); whereas the con-first group very closely resembles the control group (p-value > .35).

From a detailed analysis of the responses to each of the four attitude items shown in Table 15, it appears that responses to the items dealing with personal willingness to volunteer were not significantly influenced by the communication. Positive responses to each of the three pertinent questions were given by less than 12 per cent of subjects in each group. The differences shown by the over-all index reflect primarily the differences in responses to the item dealing with general attitude toward civil defense activity (resistance to counter-propaganda which belittled the importance of recruiting large numbers of volunteers at the present time). This item accounts for almost all of the variance between the two experimental groups.

Although the item-by-item analysis showed that neither form of the two-sided communication had any significant effect on immediate willingness to volunteer, the results, nevertheless, indicate that the sequential order of pro and con arguments made for a significant difference with respect to creating a favorable attitude toward the communicator's point of view. The outcome of the experiment supports the following conclusion concerning the effectiveness of a persuasive communication containing strong pro arguments together with weaker con arguments: The subjects receiving the pro arguments first show significantly greater acceptance of the communicator's conclusions than subjects receiving the con arguments first.

The differential effectiveness of the alternative arrangement of arguments poses a question as to whether the audience's perception of the meaning and implications of the pro and con material was influenced by the sequential context in which the material appeared. Is the greater effectiveness of the pro-first arrangement due to an "assimilation" effect, such that the con arguments tend to be seen more positively if preceded by pro arguments? For instance, when the members of an audience have just read a series of pro arguments, do they temporarily maintain such a favorable frame of mind that they simply do not notice that the con arguments present serious drawbacks?

The results from the supplementary group of 48 subjects who were given the paragraph-by-paragraph rating procedure indicates that in all probability no such assimilation effect occurred. In fact, the paragraph ratings show the opposite outcome—a general tendency toward a "contrast" effect. Subjects receiving the pro arguments first tended to give somewhat lower ratings to the con arguments than did the subjects who received the con arguments first. In other words, the con arguments were rated as being less compatible with the communicator's position when preceded by the pro arguments. Conversely, the pro arguments were rated somewhat more favorably (as supporting the communicator's position) when preceded by the con arguments. These results, then, do not support the notion that the greater effectiveness of the pro-first order can be accounted for by an assimilation effect.

Discussion

The outcome of this experiment supports the primacy hypothesis which was inferred from theoretical assumptions about the conflicting motivational tendencies aroused by pro and con arguments. In Appendix B, where the theoretical analysis is presented, a conflict model is developed on the premise that con arguments motivate an individual to reject the communicator's recommendations, whereas pro arguments motivate him in the direction of accepting the communicator's position. It is assumed that if one set of motives (tendencies to conform with the communicator's demands) is not of approximately equal strength with the competing motives (tendencies toward nonconformity), the conflict between acceptance and rejection tendencies will tend to be resolved in the direction of whichever component is stronger. If a resolution occurs before the presentation is over, the recipient will tend to be relatively unresponsive to arguments favoring the opposite position throughout the remainder of the communication. If acceptance and rejection motives are at approximately equal strengths while the communication is being presented, the longer this state of equality persists, the more strongly motivated the recipient will become to terminate the conflict. Thus during protracted periods of conflict when neither tendency predominates over the other, the recipients are most likely (a) to develop a compromise solution which attempts to reconcile the opposing positions, or (b) to attempt to escape from the conflict situation altogether by losing interest in the issue. In order to prevent conflict resolutions which are contrary to the communicator's intentions, it follows that rejection tendencies must be kept subdominant at all times during the communication exposure.

When persuasive arguments arouse both approach and avoidance tendencies, the way in which the conflict is resolved probably will play a considerable role in determining the long-run success of the communication. However, the theoretical analysis has not yet been expanded to take account of factors which influence the persistence of conflict resolution and thus pertains only to the immediate effects of conflict-arousing communications. Accordingly it must be emphasized that the present experiment provides data only on immediate reactions to a two-sided communication and was intended to throw some light only on those aspects of conflict-resolution which occur during, or shortly after, the period of communication exposure, while the contents are still salient. We interpret the findings as providing some initial empirical support for the following theoretically derived propositions concerning short-run primacy effects. When the main pro arguments are introduced first, they are in the focus of attention and operate to keep the motivation to accept at a maximal level. The con arguments are then likely to have comparatively little disruptive effect, since they tend to be outcompeted by the opposite motivational tendency. At a time when the recipient of the communication has already been powerfully stimulated to accept the conclusion being advocated, he will be most strongly disposed to ignore, discount, or reject the con arguments—even though he may be sharply aware of the fact that they contradict or argue against the communicator's position.

Our experimental findings, which show that the pro-first

order is more effective than the con-first order, would be expected to hold only under certain conditions. The theoretical assumptions from which the primacy hypothesis was derived suggest that this outcome will occur when the communication emanates from a prestigeful source, provided that the opposing arguments are not spontaneously salient, i.e. the audience is either initially unfamiliar with the con arguments or for some reason fails to recall them.

In the present experiment both the nature of the communication topic and the predispositions of the audience may have involved unspecified variables which could interact with the variables under investigation. A great deal of replication will be necessary to determine whether the same outcome occurs with different types of audiences, in other types of communication settings, and with other conflictful issues. In addition, further theoretical analysis and experimentation will be needed to study factors influencing the degree to which the short-run effects, on which the present research was focused, tend to persist after the communication contents are no longer salient and when the audience is exposed to subsequent counterpressures.

CHAPTER 9

Summary and Implications[1]

CARL I. HOVLAND

AS WE HAVE SEEN, the present volume describes an inter-related series of communication experiments designed to test a variety of theoretical formulations concerning the order in which persuasive material is presented to an audience. One set of studies tests the validity and generality of the Law of Primacy in Persuasion. This law, formulated by Lund (34), maintains that whichever side of an issue is presented first will have a greater impact on the audience than an equally strong but subsequent presentation of the opposite side. Another group of studies is primarily concerned with the effects of different sequences of appeals and arguments within a single communication. Considerable diversity of procedure and of theoretical orientation is evident in the individual studies. At this point we may abstract the general principles which emerge from the entire series of investigations and call attention to some of their implications for further research in this area.

1. The author is indebted to Rosalind L. Feierabend for a number of valuable suggestions in the writing of this chapter.

I. *Summary of Main Findings*

(1) *When two sides of an issue are presented successively by different communicators, the side presented first does not necessarily have the advantage.* Results presented on this topic in Chapter 2 raise serious questions about the generality of the Law of Primacy in Persuasion for the conditions described by Lund, in which two sides of a controversial issue are successively communicated. The study by Hovland and Mandell was originally intended to replicate the Lund experiment in all of its essential aspects as a baseline for subsequent controlled variations in conditions. Some of Lund's original topics were employed, such as the desirability of high protective tariffs for the United States. Communications successively advocating first one and then the other side of an issue were presented to the subjects to read. The order of presentation was counterbalanced, with half of the subjects receiving the affirmative arguments first and the other half the negative arguments first. Opinion questionnaires were administered after the first side and again after the second side had been presented.

Results indicated that only one of the three groups showed a greater effectiveness for the side presented first ("primacy"), while two groups showed the second side to be slightly more effective ("recency"). Since these results failed to replicate the phenomenon described by Lund, additional groups were studied using topics of greater current interest (whether antihistamines should be sold without a prescription, and whether it is feasible to build an atomic submarine [the study was done in 1949]). Three of four additional groups gave evidence that the second communication produced slightly more opinion change than the first ("recency"). In both experiments combined, a total of 548 students was studied.

These experiments are described in Chapter 2, together with an analysis of some of the factors which might be responsible for the presence or absence of primacy effects. Two classes of factors are distinguished: (1) those which affect the *learning* of the content of the first and second communications, and (2) those which influence the degree of *acceptance* of the point of view advocated in the first and second presentations. Possible artifacts entering into the Lund experiment are considered, especially the possibility that since the communicator was the subjects' regular instructor, classroom learning conditions may have been invoked when the first side of an issue was presented. When the same communicator then presented an antithetical position without any explanation, the subjects may have been confused and suspected that they were being used as subjects in an experiment, with consequent reduced effect from the second communication. This study highlights the importance of examining the conditions which produce differential effects in this area.

(2) *If, after hearing only one side of a controversial issue, a response is made which publicly indicates one's position on the issue, the effectiveness of a subsequent presentation of the second side of the issue is reduced, thus entailing a primacy effect.* Hovland, Campbell, and Brock (Chapter 3) presented one side of a controversial issue to one group of subjects and then asked them to write their opinion on the issue for publication in a magazine read by their peers. Control subjects wrote out their opinions but these were anonymous and no mention was made of possible publication. Subsequently, without prior announcement, the other side of the issue was presented to both groups and opinion measures

again secured. The authors found that the public expression of opinion tended to "freeze" the subjects' views and to make them resistant to influence by the second side of the issue.

In every-day life the greater effectiveness of the first side of an issue may sometimes be attributable to this mechanism, since an individual often makes decisions after hearing only one side of an issue and then carries out a series of acts on the basis of his decisions. Under these circumstances it may be difficult to produce a reversal of position through presentation of the opposite side of the argument.

The experimenters discuss the role of public commitment in crystallizing opinion. They believe that the effect is mediated through social rewards and the need for social approval experienced by the subjects. Having placed his views on record for others to see, the recipient may rehearse his position in anticipation of the social interaction which publication will bring. Knowledge of the social approval granted to consistency and honesty will prevent him from altering his views. Perhaps also rehearsal of his own position keeps him from paying attention to subsequent contradictory information.

(3) *The mere act of stating one's opinion anonymously on a questionnaire after hearing only one side of an issue does not significantly reduce the effectiveness of the second side.* In the study by Hovland and Mandell (Chapter 2) a comparison was made of the relative effectiveness of the first and second sides of an issue when questionnaires were interpolated between the first and second communications. Control subjects were given the first and second sides without an intervening questionnaire. The study employed the same topics as were used by Lund (34). It was thought that the intervening expression of opinion required of the experimental

subjects might have the effect of forcing them to review the arguments, to formulate their own conclusions, and to crystallize their opinion after reading only one side of the issue. This would be expected to make these subjects more resistant to a subsequent change of opinion. No such effect was found, apparently because no feeling of "commitment" was experienced under these conditions. (An incidental implication of this outcome is that the measurement process is unlikely to produce artifacts due to any commitment factor under anonymous conditions.)

(4) *When contradictory information is presented in a single communication, by a single communicator, there is a pronounced tendency for those items presented first to dominate the impression received.* This phenomenon is clearly shown in the experiments described by Luchins (Chapter 4). Two different blocks of information were prepared concerning the personality characteristics of a person not known to the subjects. One contained principally items characteristic of an extrovertive type of person and the other items characteristic of an introvertive individual. These blocks of information were given to some subjects in extrovertive-introvertive order and to others in introvertive-extrovertive order. Control groups were given only the extrovertive or the introvertive blocks. Subjects were then asked to select adjectives indicative of their impression of the individual in question. In a second experiment they were also asked to write brief personality descriptions and in the third to make predictions about later behavior and interpersonal relations of the person they had read about. It was found that the material presented first was considerably more influential than that presented second in determining what were thought to be the principal personality characteristics of the individual de-

scribed. This is in accord with Asch's findings using simple adjective lists (1). It was remarkable how many of Luchins' subjects received the incompatible information without realizing that there was any conflict of interpretation involved (over a third of a sample interviewed stated they had not been aware of any contradictions or inconsistencies).

(5) *The primacy effect found in presenting contradictory information in the same communication was reduced by interpolating other activities between the two blocks of information and by warning the subjects against the fallibility of first impressions.* These same experiments by Luchins suggested to him that the phenomenon of greater effectiveness of the first portion of a communication has many similarities to the phenomenon of "set" or "Einstellung" which he had found operative in problem-solving behavior, where the first way of attacking a problem persists throughout attempts to solve new problems (30). Some of the factors which reduce the persistence of "set" in problem solving were introduced in a replication of the primacy-recency experiment previously described. One group was run under the original conditions as a control group. A second group was explicitly warned about possible "first impression" fallacies, before any information was presented. Group three had the warning interpolated between the first and second blocks of information, and the fourth group had an arithmetic task interpolated between the two blocks of information. Sixty high school students were used in each of the four groups. Questionnaires administered at the end of the second communication concerning the personality characteristics of the person described revealed that the greater impact of the first block of information existed only for the first (control) group. For the three other groups the second block of information

tended to exert a greater influence than the first on the final impressions formed as to the personality of the individual described in the communications. The amount of "recency effect" shown for the latter groups increased progressively from group two to group four. Interpolation of the number task resulted in the greatest amount of recency effect.

(6) *Presentation of information relevant to the satisfaction of needs after these needs have been aroused brings about greater acceptance than an order which presents the information first and the need-arousal second.* Cohen compares two orders of presentation of elements within a communication: one in which a threatening situation is first created followed by information as to a possible solution, and the other in which the information is presented first and then the threat is introduced (Chapter 6). The subjects were college students, and the topic concerned the giving of course grades by grading "on the curve" (i.e. according to relative standing in class). Attitudes toward the issue were measured immediately after the communication and again three months later. The communication order which presented information relevant to need-satisfaction after those needs had been aroused brought more acceptance of the communicator's conclusion than the order which presented the information first and the need-arousal second. The difference in amount of opinion change did not appear to be associated with motivational differences, informational differences, or differences in emotional reactions to the experimental situation. Rather it appeared to be related to a perception of the information-drive arousal order as being more ambiguous than the alternative order, and relatively lacking in "cognitive clarity" and in reasonableness.

(7) *Order of presentation is a more significant factor in*

influencing opinion for subjects with relatively weak desire for understanding, than for those with "high cognitive need." Cohen measured his subjects' "cognitive need," utilizing an indicator which he and his collaborators had developed earlier (6). Distinct differences were found between subjects with high cognitive needs and those with low in the degree to which they were affected by the order in which the communicated material was presented. Subjects with high need for cognition were influenced by the communications to about the same extent, no matter what the order in which the two parts of the communication were presented. On the other hand, those with low cognitive needs were positively affected if they received the motivating material prior to the informational communication, and negatively affected if they received the two parts in reverse order. The latter subjects were, for the most part, less inclined to accept the solution if it was offered prior to their heightened anxiety over the problem. Persons with a high cognitive need, on the other hand, accept the solution whether it was presented before or after the problem was raised.

(8) *Placing communications highly desirable to the recipient first, followed by those less desirable, produces more opinion change than the reverse order.* McGuire compared two orders presented by a single communicator: one in which conclusions consonant with the desires and motives of the audience were presented first and then followed by those which were opposed to their desires, and the second in which this sequence was reversed. (Chapter 7) His hypothesis was that when the desirable items came first, the communicator would, by virtue of reinforced pairings, become progressively a stronger conditioned stimulus for eliciting responses that lead to acceptance of the positions advocated (like paying at-

tention to and learning from the communication's contents).
Conversely, responses leading to non-acceptance (e.g. with-
drawing attention) should become conditioned to the communicator who presents undesirable messages first because
agreeing with these undesirable messages is punishing. The results support the hypothesis in that the communicator elicited
more total agreement from his audience when he presented
the conclusions consonant with their desires first and the undesirable ones later, than when he presented the materials
in the reverse order. He found that subjects who received the
undesirable messages first learned the contents of the whole
series of communications less well than did those who received the desirable messages first. He interprets his results
to mean that receiving the earlier undesirable messages results in the recipient's acquiring habits interfering with the
learning of later messages by the same source (perhaps to
spare himself their anticipated unpleasant information) with
consequent reduced persuasive effect, whereas when the
earlier messages from a source have desirable contents, the
recipient acquires habits resulting in better learning of that
source's later messages, thereby augmenting their persuasiveness.

(9) *When an authoritative communicator plans to mention pro arguments and also nonsalient con arguments, the
pro-first order is superior to the con-first order.* Janis and
Feierabend examined the influence of the order in which
arguments are presented, when some of the arguments support the communicator's position and others are opposed to
it (Chapter 8). One hundred and eighty-two high school students were divided into two experimental groups and one
control group. The experimental subjects received a pamphlet which urged students to volunteer for civilian defense

activity and which contained both pro and con arguments. One of the experimental groups received a version of the pamphlet in which the pro arguments were presented first, followed by the con arguments; the second group received a version in which this order was reversed. The control group received no relevant communication. A postcommunication questionnaire on willingness to volunteer for civil defense activity was used to test the relative effectiveness of the two forms of the communication. The group receiving pro arguments first consistently expressed more favorable attitudes than both the group receiving the con arguments first and the control group. Significant differences were found on a combined index of attitude toward volunteering for Civil Defense work based on four questionnaire items.

The results are interpreted in terms of the resolution of an approach-avoidance conflict (Appendix B). At the outset the recipient is favorably disposed toward the communicator and motivated to accept his conclusions. Provided the opposing negative arguments are not spontaneously salient, hearing pro arguments strengthens this approach tendency to the point where later con arguments can be accepted without causing the recipient to reverse his initially favorable position. When the con arguments are given at the outset, however, an avoidance tendency is established which the later pro arguments are not capable of reversing.

II. *Implications for Further Research*

The preceding results raise a host of problems for further research. One which has been little investigated involves systematic exploration of the relationship between primacy effects and the degree to which the individual is already familiar with the issue. In most of the experiments herein reported, as well as in the study by Lund, it is probable that some prior knowledge existed on the topic under discussion. As we have seen, under these conditions a law of primacy does not seem to be a valid general principle. But it may be that when no prior knowledge of the topic is involved, a law of primacy does operate. The factor of familiarity was actually invoked by Lund to explain one of his groups which failed to show much influence: "Propositions upon which one has already had ample opportunity to form an opinion should be much less subject to persuasive influence" (34, p. 189).

This problem suggests that further attention must be given to the appropriate specification of conditions for the operation of a law of primacy. Should primacy be defined as the very first presentation of unknown material to an audience, or is it simply the first portion of any communicated material regardless of the recipient's familiarity with the issue? Rarely is the communicator in a position to be the first to address his audience on a particular subject. Some degree of prior familiarity with almost any topic must be assumed both in experimental and in real-life situations. What then is the practical definition of primacy in experimental studies? Since it cannot claim to represent the first material ever presented on the issue, it is generally limited to the first portion of the material in question.

The results of the present series of studies seem to suggest that the nearer one comes to achieving primacy in the sense of the first presentation of unfamiliar material, the more apt one is to obtain primacy effects. Undoubtedly the material least familiar to the recipient is found in Luchins' studies on forming impressions of personality. Thus in this case the subject was asked to form an impression of an unknown person based upon information which was presented for the first time. Undoubtedly further research bearing directly on the relationship between prior familiarity with the topic under discussion and the relative effectiveness of the side of the issue presented first would greatly help to clarify the extent of generality of a law of primacy.

One of the effects of such prior familiarity with an issue is to alert one to the fact that there may be conflicting points of view involved. Thus this factor is closely related to the results of Luchins, which show that lack of awareness of conflict is associated with the appearance of primacy effects. It is also closely related to salience considerations discussed by Janis and Feierabend (Appendix B). One of the major factors determining spontaneous salience is prior familiarity with the arguments. Familiarity with an issue thus helps to determine whether the set of arguments presented first will be in the favored position.

The apparent differences between their results favoring the presentation of pro arguments first, and those of Hovland, Lumsdaine, and Sheffield (19), who found it desirable to introduce negative arguments early to assure the hearer who is opposed initially that his own position was being taken into account, may be due to the difference in salience of the negative arguments. In the Janis and Feierabend situation the audience was first introduced to the negative arguments by the communication. The objections were not spontaneously salient. In the Hovland, Lumsdaine, and Sheffield experiment, on the other hand, the hearers who were more favorably influenced by the two-sided argument were already acutely aware of some of the arguments against the communicator's position and were actively considering them. Under these circumstances the authors recommended mentioning the opposed arguments at the outset and also deliberately answering them. A critical experiment is suggested in which the salience of the opposing arguments is systematically varied or compared, to test the interaction hypothesis that with high initial salience the early introduction of negative arguments is desirable, while when the opposing arguments are not salient it is better to develop the positive arguments before introducing the negative ones.

Awareness of incompatibility might be expected to depend to some extent upon whether two communicators are involved or only a single one presents the contradictory material. This is an important research problem which has not yet been attacked. In the present series of experiments the results are compatible with the hypothesis that primacy is less when the two sides of an issue are presented by different communicators. Thus in the Luchins study, and in the experiments by McGuire and by Janis and Feierabend, primacy effects were obtained. These investigations all involved a single communicator. It will also be recalled that only a single communicator was involved in the Lund study. On the other hand, different communicators presented the alternate sides of the argument in the Hovland and Mandell experiment and in the control condition of the Hovland, Campbell, and Brock study, and in neither of these were primacy effects obtained. What is needed, however, is systematic experimentation in which one holds constant the topics, subjects, and other factors while a single communicator versus two opposed communicators is compared. Only studies set up specifically to test these hypotheses can establish the validity of the generalizations suggested on the basis of naturalistic variations which occurred in the studies herein reported.

A closely related research problem concerns the expectation of the recipient that a second side will be presented subsequently. Where there is an awareness that there are two sides of the issue to be presented there may be a tendency not to make up one's mind on the basis of the side which comes first but to wait until both sides have been presented. On the other hand, when the recipient expects that only one side will be presented, he may make up his mind on the basis of the side presented first and even take actions which commit him to the position he initially adopts. In the studies by Hovland and Mandell and by Hovland, Campbell, and Brock using alternate presentations of the two sides, no mention was made at the time of commitment that a second communication giving the other side would follow. An interesting experiment is suggested in which there would be systematic variation of the factor of expectation of refutation, with half of the subjects being told that the other side would be presented later and half not being told the second side would be forthcoming. If the subjects anticipate counterargument, it is possible that they will hold off accepting the first position, adopting a neutral or compromise position in order to avoid the conflict that comes from subsequently finding their own opinion at marked variance with the impressive views of a prestigeful communicator (in a manner closely related to the Janis-Feierabend formulation).

Another factor which probably plays an important role in determining the extent of primacy effects in real-life communications is the likelihood of subsequent exposure to the "other side" of an issue. In the experiments reported in this volume we were dealing with classroom situations where we could guarantee some exposure to both sides of the issue being studied. In many situations we do not have any control over exposure. Under these circumstances it is highly prob-

able that one of the effects of primacy is to reduce the likelihood of self-exposure to the second side. In many situations
of daily life primacy is important because the individual who
has once acquired information, a mode of perception, or a
new attitude thereafter does not permit himself to be exposed to contradictory information. While experiments dealing with naturalistic situations are notoriously difficult, we
have suggested elsewhere (17, p. 1099) the need for a line of
research in which results obtained in experiments with captive audiences are compared with those obtaining where self-
exposure is involved.

The effects of various types of committing action in "freezing" opinion after a communication need considerable further investigation. In one of the present studies significantly
fewer subjects changed their position when exposed to a second communication after they had expressed their opinion
publicly (Chapter 3). When the expression of opinion was
anonymous, no decrease was obtained (Chapter 2). These results might be interpreted by some as indicating greater effectiveness of public as compared with private commitment.
But actually in neither of the present studies was an attempt
made to have the subjects regard their expression of opinion
as a commitment. Would such an attempt have increased the
"fixation" of opinion after the first side was presented, and
would there have been a difference between public and private commitment in this respect (cf. 3, 8, 12)? These are questions for future research. An incidental finding on commitment effects obtained in the experiment by Hovland, Campbell, and Brock may merit follow-up. There was a suggestion
in their data that the effect of the *first* communication is reduced when subjects are asked to express their opinions publicly after hearing it. This effect was not statistically signifi-

cant in their study and was only a serendipidous finding, but it should be studied as a phenomenon in its own right. If operative, it would counterbalance the tendency for commitment to reduce the effect of the second communication, and manifest itself as a reduction in extent of fluctuation in successive measurements of opinion response under "commitment" as compared to "no commitment" conditions.

In the majority of the experiments in this volume only a short time interval elapsed between the two conflicting communications. Interpolation of time intervals between the two contradictory blocks of information was shown by Luchins to be a factor which reduced the extent of primacy effects (within the rather narrow range of times he studied), possibly because it alerted the reader to potential disparity in the material. On the other hand, interpolation of time also permits an individual to take actions on the basis of hearing only one side of an issue which may subsequently commit him to the position chosen, and this might increase primacy effects (Chapter 3). How will these two factors interact in group situations of the type with which we must sometimes be concerned? Only systematic research varying the time interval between the two conflicting communications can provide definitive answers to such questions. Studies on temporal effects in associative and reproductive interference in learning suggest some interesting hypotheses for investigation (cf. *Communication and Persuasion,* chapter 4). They also highlight the need for studies in which the time interval between the two communications and the measures of effect is varied. The incidental findings of Cohen concerning the delayed effect on opinion of different attitudes toward the communicator are relevant to this question and fit in well with the findings on a sleeper effect in the study by Hovland and Weiss

(21). Such studies may help to bridge the sizeable gap between the formulations derived from simple verbal material and the generalizations obtaining with complex persuasive messages.

Very little research has been conducted to date on the problem of the relationship between the organization of the communication and the personality characteristics of the recipient. The results of Cohen, in Chapter 6, show that the effect of order of presentation is less for those of his subjects who have high cognitive needs. It may be that persons with low need for cognition are influenced predominantly by the material which reaches them first, particularly if emotional or motivational factors are brought into play such that the material provides some particular need satisfaction. Individuals with high need for cognition, however, may be capable of taking all bits of information into account, regardless of whether the information is the first or last to come to their attention. It would be interesting to find that the relationship studied here could be more widely generalized to indicate that organizational factors are less important in general for persons with a high cognitive need, implying that such persons are themselves capable of rearranging elements in the most appropriate order regardless of the initial presentation. A good situation for this type of extension might be in connection with the problem studied by Janis and Feierabend. The prediction could be made that starting with the pro arguments would be important in the case of low-cognitive need subjects but that high-cognitive need subjects would be apt to pursue the discussion to the end even when con arguments were introduced early and hence be little affected by order of presentation.

An obvious type of extension of research on personality

variables would be replication of some of our experiments on other types of populations. All of our studies were done with either high school or college students in America. When we see the extent of individual differences within this narrow range, our attention is called to the possible importance of age, sex, and national differences. We should certainly expect that whatever complex of personality characteristics is measured by Cohen's test of "cognitive need" would be expected to be highly variable when other populations are involved. Undoubtedly individuals with little education will on the average have lower interest in thorough comprehension of issues and hence should be more influenced by order of presentation than those from the populations studied by us in educational institutions.

Many other interesting problems remain as regards the primacy-recency controversy. To mention one final problem let us consider an implication of primacy effects for refutation of arguments suggested by Lund. He writes: "The speaker or writer engaged in a debate or dealing with a controversial subject, in observing the importance of primacy, should not follow the climax order in presenting his argument, but should weaken sympathy with his opponent *promptly* by attacking his strongest argument first, thus lessening the force of his adversary's case as quickly as possible" (34, p. 190). Does this mean that it is more effective to give strong refutation to impress the audience with the fallacy of the opponent before trying to establish the truth of one's own position? If so, this is not a direct implication of the principle of primacy. The principle does not specify whether or not it would be most effective to begin with refutation. Without this specification it is not always clear how the law of primacy should be utilized, even if it exists. But the above quotation nevertheless suggests an interesting area of research, that of examining the interrelationship between primacy factors and effective refutation of arguments.

III. *Some Unsolved Theoretical Problems*

Throughout the monograph, a number of different theoretical factors have been invoked to explain the results of the various experiments. Luchins, for example, utilizes the concept of "set" or "Einstellung" in accounting for the operation of primacy in forming impressions of personality. He believes that the first presented material establishes a set which serves as a frame of reference into which later information is fitted. This set operates to reduce awareness of conflict and causes the material which is presented first to color whatever subsequent material the communicatee may receive on the same subject. He is thus able to relate the operation of primacy to the operation of set in problem-solving, where prior experience with one method of reaching a solution persists in attempts to solve new problems, even though it may be an inefficient method. It is often found in problem solving studies that interpolating other tasks between the problems and also warning the subjects in advance against the persistence of set tends to reduce that very persistence. Luchins accordingly used these methods in an attempt to minimize primacy effects and found the same procedures effective.

McGuire utilizes a stimulus-response learning analysis to explain the fact that the responses made to a first set of materials have a disproportionate effect on later behavior. In this analysis of the communication-persuasion process the source and message components of the communication are identified as the stimuli and the relevant responses are considered to be the chain of stimulus-producing responses (e.g.

attention, comprehension, etc.) which culminate in the recipients' agreement or disagreement with the position advocated in the communication. When the source's earlier messages advocate positions in line with the recipients' desires, that source tends to become a conditioned stimulus for eliciting the chain of responses that culminates in agreement with his position, since whenever the recipient does perform this chain of responses, he is led to accept a position he finds desirable, i.e. he is reinforced. When, on the other hand, the source's earlier messages advocate positions which the recipients find undesirable, the recipients are in effect put in an "avoidance training" situation in which they learn to avoid paying attention to, or understanding, the source's positions, thus avoiding the painful experience of having to accept a position which they regard as undesirable. Hence, it is important when a single source transmits a series of messages, some with desirable content and some with undesirable, that the desirable precede the undesirable so as to retain the attention of the recipients.

The third theoretical formulation is that of "conflict theory." Janis and Feierabend suggest that the pro arguments in a communication develop approach tendencies toward the position of the communicator, while con arguments invoke avoidance tendencies. Thus an approach-avoidance conflict is created when both sides of an issue are presented. Hearing pro arguments at the outset strengthens the approach tendency to the point where later con arguments can be accepted without causing the recipient to reverse his initial approach responses. Should the con arguments be given first, however, an avoidance tendency is established which the later pro arguments are not capable of overcoming.

The interesting question remains as to what extent any

one of these theoretical formulations can subsume the phenomena initially covered by a different theoretical outlook,
and to what extent it makes unique predictions of outcome.
Is it possible, for example, to explain the results of Cohen's
experiment by using the stimulus-response analysis suggested
by McGuire? It will be recalled that Cohen compared one
situation in which threatening material preceded the giving
of information concerning a solution and another in which
the reverse order was employed. The former was the more
effective. In stimulus-response terms, it would be said that
learning is superior when the response to be learned is followed by a reduction in the strength of a drive. In this situation it would mean that when little anxiety was present (low
drive) there would be little drive reduction associated with
the learning of the information presented. But when the
threatening material was presented first, drive would be increased and would then be reduced by the information offering a possible solution. Consequently favorable conditions
would be established for the acquisition of the message.
Cohen's discussion in terms of need arousal and satisfaction
is closely parallel at this point to the stimulus-response formulation utilized by McGuire.

It might be tempting to assume that the Janis-Feierabend
and the McGuire results can be readily combined into a single theoretical formulation. Equating McGuire's "desirable
outcomes" with Janis and Feierabend's "pro arguments"
would lead to the generalization that positive (desirable) incentives should be presented before negative (undesirable)
incentives. There are undoubtedly some conditions under
which this equating of terms would be justifiable and the
same outcome predicted for substantially the same theoretical reason. But there need not be a direct correspondence be-

tween pro arguments and desirable outcomes under all experimental conditions. The relationship may even be a negative one if the communicator is advocating a position opposed to that initially held by the recipient. Under such circumstances con arguments (i.e. those leading to a conclusion contrary to that advocated by the communicator) may be consonant with the individual's own position and hence something which he very much wants to believe. This is illustrated in the study by Hovland, Lumsdaine, and Sheffield (19, chapter 8); although the communication argued that the war with Japan would take a long time, one of the negative arguments initially held by members of the audience was that it would be a short war, since Japan was so weak. This negative argument was definitely one which the audience wanted to believe.

It would be interesting to explore the possibility of differential predictions arising from the conditioning model used by McGuire and from the conflict model employed by Janis and Feierabend. What would be the outcome if the factors postulated by the two systems were pitted against each other in such a way that the first set of arguments in the communications was entirely of a desirable character but was opposed to the position advocated by the communicator? McGuire would predict increased attention to the communicator under such conditions, with consequent greater persuasiveness when the undesirable conclusions were subsequently introduced. Janis and Feierabend would foresee the development of avoidance tendencies which would interfere with the acceptance of the communicator's positive message. If the factors highlighted by the two theories should both be operative, their effects might cancel each other. One would then need to place greater emphasis on separate interaction hypotheses, in order to specify the conditions under which various factors would produce one or the other outcome.

The question also arises as to whether the Einstellung formulation suggested by Luchins to explain his primacy-recency experiments might also apply to the Janis and Feierabend and McGuire results. His theory claims that whatever set is induced by the first presentation will carry over into a second set of materials unless something is done to disrupt the set. In the Janis-Feierabend experiment the set would be one of agreeing with the arguments presented first, and this would then dominate the final conclusion. If the first ones were pro arguments, acceptance of the communicator's conclusion would result; if they were con, rejection would be expected. In the McGuire experiment Luchins' formulation would imply that the tendency to pay attention to and accept the communicator's position which is generated by the initial set of desirable messages would persist if desirable conclusions were presented first, and the opposite effect would result if the order were reversed.

Again the crucial question is not whether the phenomena are uniquely predicted by a particular theoretical system but whether the various theories call attention to different aspects of the problem and give rise to differential predictions under changed conditions. In the present instance it is possible that differential predictions would be made should the temporal conditions be altered. Explanations in terms of set require immediately successive conditions for maximum effect. If a time interval were introduced between the first and the second halves of the communications in the McGuire or Janis-Feierabend studies, Luchins would of necessity predict lessened primacy effects. The other experimenters do not specify the nature of the relevant time interval, hence one should not expect it to be of major importance in their formulation. If the introduction of a time interval or the interpolation of another task was of major effect, it would require that something be added to the McGuire and Janis-Feierabend system. Should their phenomenon persist even with a long interpolated delay, Luchins might be forced to specify the manner in which sets are re-established and reinstated. He might thus turn to similar formulations in terms of facilitation and interference effects and be subsequently led to more comprehensive formulations covering both sets of data. An interesting attempt along these lines, of relating conflict theory to experiments on impressions of personality, has recently been made by Pepitone and Hayden (38).

In any case it is clear that crucial experiments pitting one theoretical approach against another lie in the future of communication research. What we see as present is that the various formulations bring to bear, in analyzing the problem, a set of considerations which might never have been considered if only a single system were employed. Thus factors minimizing set, derived from prior studies of problem solving, are tested in relation to the field of organization of impressions of personality by Luchins. The nature of the relation between various motives and the informational elements of a communication is suggested by Cohen, who thus alerts us to individual differences in desire and ability to organize experiences. The role of communication order in capturing and maintaining attention is stressed by McGuire, and the importance of minimizing conflict by guaranteeing an overriding positive response at all times during a communication is highlighted by Janis and Feierabend. Undoubtedly each formulation could be elaborated to account for the findings of the others, but at the present time they have not been developed to this stage. Each calls to our attention a somewhat different set of relevant factors. Nevertheless we look forward to the day when a more comprehensive theoretical system is developed which will unify the present disparate phenomena and explorations.

IV. *General Implications*

The implications of the results derived from the experiments on arrangement and organization within a single communication are relatively straightforward. The experiment by Cohen stresses the need for arousing desire and concern before suggesting appropriate action. This is a practice often followed by successful intuitive practitioners of the art of communication (cf. 4) but frequently forgotten in everyday situations where solutions are often suggested without adequate prior establishment of the need for the action recommended. It is possible that preparation is not essential when the recipient is highly motivated and intellectually concerned, but is critical for the members of an audience whose cognitive needs are low. At least that is one implication of Cohen's results on personality differences.

McGuire's results suggest the desirability of putting early on the agenda those issues toward which members of an audience are initially favorable, to increase the likelihood of developing interest and attention. This procedure is also in line with the implication of the Janis-Feierabend study of not raising opposing arguments until enough pro arguments have been given to achieve a predominantly favorable situation for consideration of the con side of the issue. The practical implication of taking the initial attitudes and knowledge of the audience fully into account is, however, often neglected. The results of Janis and Feierabend, taken in conjunction with those of Hovland, Lumsdaine, and Sheffield, suggest that what is an appropriate order for one type of audience may be inappropriate for another. Specifically the results of the two experiments taken together suggest that when the objections to the position being advocated are not salient it is better to start with the arguments supporting one's position, but where the recipient is already highly aware of the opposed arguments it is better to acknowledge them promptly and discuss them at the point where they are apt to arise in his mind. These implications are clearly opposed to a principle often applied of avoiding all reference to the opposition—cf. Dunlap's rule: "Do not admit there is any 'other side' " (11, p. 360). Presumably this principle depends on the recipient's never being exposed to the other side.

The general picture which emerges from the experiments in which both sides of an issue are presented successively is that concern as to the danger of first impressions becoming lasting impressions is probably exaggerated, at least for situations where representatives of both sides have an opportunity to present their views. The public is not necessarily permanently swayed by the view to which it first lends an ear, or biased by the man who first captures its attention.

The present group of experiments indicate the conditions under which the danger of the first side's prevailing is likely to be pronounced and also permit some specification of procedures which minimize such a danger. The combined findings from all of the different studies reported suggest that the side of an issue presented first is likely to have a disproportionate influence on opinion under the following conditions: (1) when cues as to the incompatibility of different items of information are absent, (2) when the contradictory information is presented by the same communicator, (3) when committing actions are taken after only one side of the issue has been presented, (4) when the issue is an unfamiliar one, and (5) when the recipient has only a superficial interest in the issue (low cognitive need). When one deals with situations in which exposure to both sides cannot be assumed, but where the recipient himself controls whether he will expose himself to the second side after hearing the first, additional factors favoring primacy become involved (27, 28).

For important social situations in which primacy effects have been considered a danger, for example, legal trials, election campaigns and political debates, the issue is usually clearly defined as controversial, the partisanship of the communicator is established and different communicators present the opposing sides. These factors should give rise to relatively little primacy effect. Our concern might then be concentrated on preventing premature commitment on the basis of the first presentation alone and on developing interest and responsibility on the part of the citizen to insure objectivity and a genuine desire to reach the heart of the issue.

There are other situations, however, in which the dangers of primacy effect are very real. The deliberate use of primacy for propagandistic effect has already been mentioned (cf. p. 6). It is frequently effective under conditions where the controversial nature of the issue is not mentioned, where early commitment is sought, and where exposure to other points of view is minimized, either through self-selection of exposure or through monopoly control of information (27). Totalitarian regimes deliberately utilize commitment effects to prevent the "other side" from having its influence, by requiring persons attending political meetings to make public expression of their views as well as to listen to the views of others.

In free countries, on the other hand, effort is made to prevent individuals who are being exposed to controversial material from taking any action before the other side is presented. Wise advisors frequently tell the individual "Don't say 'Yes' or 'No' now but think it over" so that both pro and con considerations can be taken into account. Even anonymous straw votes may serve to "freeze" opinion prematurely, although probably not to the extent expressed by Lund. At least that seems to be the implication of the study by Hovland and Mandell, where anonymous expression of opinion on a questionnaire was insufficient to produce primacy effects.

Primacy may frequently operate also in forming impressions of personality, where the present results are consonant with the popular belief about first impressions. Here bits of information about personality and behavior accumulate slowly over time. When there is no initial indication that the data may be incompatible considerable primacy prevails (Chapter 4). This situation is one in which the educational process must play a role in warning individuals against the fallacy of deciding on the basis of only limited evidence. Such procedures are shown by Luchins to be quite effective (Chapter 5). Presumably other methods used in eliminating "halo effects" in judgment might also be applicable.

Undue influence of early observations may sometimes create difficulties in scientific work. Typically the researcher extracts items of information from nature through experimentation and observation. Some of these are consonant with one theory and others with another. The impression formed by early observations and protocols may persist even when no longer compatible with new evidence, in the absence of clear-cut cues as to the incompatibility of the different findings.

Commitment may also be a factor of concern in the example of the scientist just described. It will be recalled that it was found that when subjects indicated publicly their position on an issue after only a single side had been presented, they were less apt to take the other side into account when it was subsequently discussed. If the scientific investigator quickly fits his early findings into a theoretical framework on the basis of some hunch, he may be reluctant to relinquish his views in the face of nonconfirming instances. This act of theory construction might be considered analagous to public commitment. The scientist, having committed himself, albeit privately, is apt to regard all subsequent data from within his adopted theoretical framework, often discounting later facts which come to his attention. Bias in scientific inquiry thus produced may impede rational theory construction. An important part of the training of a scientist consists of learning to suspend judgment until all the facts have come to light, to be particularly on the look-out for incompatible evidence, and to avoid becoming emotionally involved in the maintenance of one's own particular theories.

Finally, there are interesting implications of the personality results cited by Cohen. Individuals with high "cognitive needs" resisted the effect of primacy to a considerable extent. Was this a product of education and training, or of personality differences arising early in life? Study of this factor could shed considerable light on the process whereby objectivity is produced and have applicability for scientists, jurists and even the average citizen in his everyday dealings with others in the community. Here lies a real challenge for education and training.

The Representation of Order Effects in Communication Research

NORMAN H. ANDERSON AND CARL I. HOVLAND

IN EXPERIMENTS modeled after those of Lund (34) in which two sides of an issue are presented successively, a primacy effect is said to occur when the amount of change produced by the communication presented first (regardless of which side it argues for) exceeds that produced by the one presented second, and a recency effect when the change produced by the second exceeds that brought about by the first. (To counterbalance possible differences in the persuasiveness of the two communications themselves, in experiments one subgroup is usually given the pro communication first, and another subgroup the con first. In these introductory paragraphs, however, it will be convenient to assume that the pro and con communications have equal effectiveness, meaning that either presented in first position will produce the same magnitude of change.) The implied reference point in such experiments is one in which neither primacy nor recency operates, and the recipient is moved a certain distance by the first communication and then moved back an equal distance by the second so that his final and initial attitudes are the same. Primacy and recency effects are then interpreted as arising from some change in susceptibility of the recipient, e.g. commitment, "set," etc.

Such a formulation implicitly sets up the following representation of communication effects: the attitude of any particular recipient after receiving a communication is described as his initial attitude plus a change score attributable to the communication. Applying this formulation to the primacy-recency problem, the recipient's attitude after the first—say, pro—communication may be expressed as

$$X_1 = X_0 + d_1.$$

Similarly, after hearing both the first and the second (con) communications, the recipient's attitude may be written as

$$X_2 = X_1 + d_2.$$

Here X_0 is the original position of this recipient along the opinion continuum, X_1 his attitude after receiving the first (pro) communication, X_2 his attitude after receiving the pro, and then the con communication, and d_1 and d_2 are the changes effected by the first and second communications, respectively.

This representation may be used in a straightforward empirical way to exhibit the observed data. However, we are here interested in the implications of this formulation for order effects. If d_1 and d_2 are equal in magnitude, then the two changes cancel (being opposite in sign), leaving $X_2 = X_0$. This is then the reference base-line for primacy-recency effects in this mode of representation of communication effects. Primacy or recency effects, reflected in differences in the magnitudes of d_1 and d_2, would then be credited to the operation of changes in susceptibility from the first to the second presentations.

However, a number of recent studies have indicated that the amount of change produced by a communication tends to be proportional to the amount of change attempted (12, 13, 14, 20). The formulation suggested by these authors, that the opinion change effected is proportional to the total advocated change, may be expressed as follows:

$$X_1 = X_0 + S(C - X_0), \qquad (1)$$

where X_0 is the initial attitude

X_1 is the attitude after administration of the communication

C is the position of the communication on the attitude continuum

S is a proportionality factor.

This may be called the distance-proportional, or linear, representation. It gives the change in attitude as the proportion S of the distance, $C - X_0$, between the recipient and the communication. S will be called susceptibility to influence: when $S = 0$, the recipient is unaffected by the communication; as S takes on larger and larger positive values, the recipient is moved more and more in the direction of the communication; if S is negative, the recipient is influenced away from the communication.

To illustrate how this would operate in a pro-con presentation, it will be assumed that the initial attitude of the recipient is 5; that the position of the con communication is 2, and that of the pro communication 8, on the attitude continuum; and that each communication moves the recipient halfway from his current position toward the position of the communication presented (i.e. with no change in susceptibility to influence). Then after presenting the pro communication, the new attitude will be

$$X_1 = 5 + \tfrac{1}{2}(8 - 5) = 6.50; \quad \text{change} = +1.50.$$

Presenting now the con communication, the new attitude will be

$$X_2 = 6.5 + \tfrac{1}{2}(2 - 6.5) = 4.25; \quad \text{change} = -2.25.$$

The corresponding values for the subjects given the con-pro order would be

$$X_1 = 5 + \tfrac{1}{2}(2 - 5) = 3.50; \quad \text{change} = -1.50.$$
$$X_2 = 3.5 + \tfrac{1}{2}(8 - 3.5) = 5.75; \quad \text{change} = +2.25.$$

An important implication for the problem of order effects is readily seen. With no change in susceptibility of the recipient (e.g. no commitment effect, no increased attentiveness, etc.), we should *not* anticipate that the two communication effects will cancel as in the previous representation. Rather, it is to be expected that a recency effect (as defined above) will be produced. In everyday language we might say that this comes about because the first communication has increased the distance between the recipient and the second communication which, accordingly, has a greater potential influence.

Although we have used quite a special illustrative example, the result remains the same under fairly general circumstances: on the base-line of no change in susceptibility to persuasive influence, the distance-proportional representation of communication effects implies that a recency effect will obtain. This will be shown in the formal development of this representation to be given below.

It is thus seen that these two ways of representing communications lead to different expectations with regard to order effects. The representation ordinarily employed takes a zero order effect as the base-line reference, with any observed primacy or recency effects to be interpreted as caused by changes in susceptibility. In the distance-proportional representation, a base-line with some recency effect is involved, and deviations therefrom are in need of interpretation or explanation. It will be observed that these two formulations entail somewhat different definitions of susceptibility.

The distance-proportional representation has the advantage of being in accord with the recent experiments mentioned above. It may also be supported by the following consideration of a more formal nature. Consider two pro communications, each so effective that either presented first would move the recipient more than half way toward the pro position. Then the communication presented second necessarily produces a smaller change than the one presented initially. The first representation would then *automatically* imply a change in susceptibility. However, this conclusion would not be obligatory in the distance-proportional representation where the second communication would be expected to produce a smaller magnitude change since the distance between the recipient and the communication has been decreased. Against the distance-proportional formulation is the fact that it requires an empirical determination of the base-line order effect, whereas the other mode of representation assigns it the a priori value of zero.

Neither formulation can be considered as compelling at the present stage of inquiry, and only future work can determine their relative usefulness. It is hoped that this note will stimulate research to provide the empirical basis needed for evaluation of these and other approaches to the analytical representation of communications and their effects.

We turn now to the formal development of the order effect using the linear, or distance-proportional, representation introduced above. It will be assumed that we are dealing with a single attitude, or opinion, measured as a continuous variable on a unidimensional scale.

Consider first a single communication. On the assumption that change in attitude is a continuous function of initial attitude, it follows that there is some attitude which is left unchanged by the communication. This attitude will be denoted by C and we shall speak of it as the fixed point of the communication. The fixed point is a characteristic parameter of the communication and may be thought of as the position of the communication-communicator combination on the attitude continuum. It gives a more precise description of the communication than does a label of pro or con. Thus a weak pro and a strong pro communication would (presumably) have different fixed points. It should be noted that the fixed point is operationally defined with respect to the behavior of the population under consideration.

Taking the change in attitude to be proportional to the distance between the recipient and the communication, the effect of the communication is written as before:

$$X_1 = X_0 + S(C - X_0), \tag{1}$$

where X_0 is the initial attitude of some particular recipient, X_1 the attitude after the communication, C the fixed point of the communication, and S the proportionality factor.

The value of S governs the amount and direction of change. When $S = 0$, the recipient is uninfluenced by the communication; for $S > 0$, the recipient moves toward C; when $S = 1$, the new attitude is identical with the position of the communication; when $S > 1$, the recipient "overshoots" C; and, finally, for $S < 0$, the recipient is influenced away from the position of the communication, producing a "boomerang" effect. Of course, if $C = X_0$, then equation 1 states that no change is produced which is consistent with the definition of fixed point.

It should be explicitly realized that S is not a constant. It will certainly depend on X_0, since it is a matter of common observation that the more extreme attitudes are held more intensely. It will depend as well on other personality variables not indexed by X. The relation between the communicator and the recipient will also influence the value of S, depending, in particular, on the valuation of the communicator and the "power" of the communicator over the recipient. Thus S is still a gross variable, in need of further analysis and reduction. However, in the specific application of this formulation to the primacy-recency problem, in which the same communications and communicators are used both in first and second positions, many of these factors will counterbalance out, and it seems reasonable to interpret S simply as susceptibility to change.

It should also be observed that equation 1 is not a hypothesis in the ordinary sense; rather, it constitutes a definition of the S function as it depends on initial attitude. For, since C, X_0, and X_1 may be determined empirically, S is just that function which is needed to make equation 1 true at each value of X_0. Such a procedure may seem somewhat surprising, although it is perhaps more common than is ordinarily realized (e.g. the notion of force in Lewinian psychology, or of drive in Hullian theory). In the absence of external quantification, it is not possible to make a more substantive hypothesis. However, it seems reasonable to expect that the S

values so obtained will not be inconsistent with common usage, but instead exceed it in exactness.

To apply the linear representation of equation 1 to the order effect problem, we now consider two communications, A and B. By relabeling if necessary, we may always take the fixed point, C_a, of A to be less than the fixed point, C_b, of B, so that C_a lies to the left of C_b on the attitude continuum. The discussion will be restricted to the case where the initial attitude lies between C_a and C_b, and where the S values lie between 0 and 1. These restrictions seem reasonable for most primacy-recency experiments and are made to avoid certain special cases which require a more detailed investigation. However, equations 2 through 11 are valid without these restrictions.

In keeping track of the attitudes as affected by the applications of these communications, the following notation is used:

X_0 = some particular initial attitude,
X_a = attitude after presentation of A,
X_b =   "   "   "   " B,
X_{ab} =   "   "   "   " A followed by B,
X_{ba} =   "   "   "   " B "   " A.

Furthermore, to provide for possible unequal effectiveness of the two communications, it is necessary to use different susceptibility factors, S_a and S_b, for A and B, respectively. Then, for the initial presentation,

$$X_a = X_0 + S_a(C_a - X_0), \text{ if } A \text{ is applied first,} \quad (2)$$

and

$$X_b = X_0 + S_b(C_b - X_0), \text{ if } B \text{ is applied first.} \quad (3)$$

In representing the effect of the second communication, the possibility must be allowed that the S values and the fixed points of the communications will have changed in consequence of the first communication. Using the same system of subscript notation, let

S_{ab} = susceptibility to B, after A has been applied
S_{ba} = susceptibility to A, " B " " "
C_{ab} = fixed point of B, " A " " "
C_{ba} = fixed point of A, " B " " "

Then the final attitudes after the two orders of presentation are

$$X_{ab} = X_a + S_{ab}(C_{ab} - X_a), \qquad (4)$$
$$X_{ba} = X_b + S_{ba}(C_{ba} - X_b). \qquad (5)$$

We now define the order effect, $\triangle(X)$, as the difference between the final attitudes resulting under the two orders of presentation:

$$\triangle(X_0) = X_{ab} - \dot{X}_{ba}. \qquad (6)$$

A positive order effect is a recency effect. For, if $\triangle(X_0) > 0$, then X_{ab} lies to the right of X_{ba} on the attitude continuum. Recalling that C_b lies to the right of C_a, it is seen that when a positive order effect obtains, the communicator of B would prefer to act second, since the final attitude would then be X_{ab}. In the same way, the communicator of A would also desire to act second, since the final attitude would then be X_{ba}, which lies to the left of X_{ab} and hence closer to C_a. A negative order effect is a primacy effect and may be given an analogous geometrical interpretation.

In order to obtain an explicit expression for $\triangle(X_0)$, equations 2 and 3 are substituted in equations 4 and 5 to yield

$$X_{ab} = X_0 + S_a(C_a - X_0) + S_{ab}[C_{ab} - X_0 - S_a(C_a - X_0)] \quad (7)$$
$$X_{ba} = X_0 + S_b(C_b - X_0) + S_{ba}[C_{ba} - X_0 - S_b(C_b - X_0)] \quad (8)$$

Substituting these expressions in equation 6 gives

$$\triangle(X_0) = (C_b - X_0)(S_bS_{ba} - S_b) - (C_a - X_0)(S_aS_{ab} - S_a)$$
$$+ S_{ab}(C_{ab} - X_0) - S_{ba}(C_{ba} - X_0) \quad (9)$$

This is the most general expression for the order effect, subject only to the three assumptions used in its derivation: (1) that equation 1 holds; (2) that the fixed points of the communications exist; and (3) that the attitude is measured on some continuous unidimensional scale. For working purposes, we now make the further assumption that any changes in the fixed points may be neglected, so that $C_a = C_{ba}$, and $C_b = C_{ab}$, although this may be hazardous and should be investigated empirically. With a little algebra, equation 9 then becomes

$$\triangle(X_0) = (C_b - X_0)[S_{ba}S_b - (S_b - S_{ab})]$$
$$- (C_a - X_0)[S_{ab}S_a - (S_a - S_{ba})] \quad (10)$$

Now the reference base-line of no change in susceptibility to influence means that $S_b = S_{ab}$, and $S_a = S_{ba}$. Making the corresponding substitutions in equation 10, the base-line order effect becomes

$$\triangle(X_0) = (C_b - X_0)S_aS_b - (C_a - X_0)S_bS_a$$
$$= S_aS_b(C_b - C_a). \quad (11)$$

This base-line order effect depends on the product of the distance between (the fixed points of) the two communications and the two susceptibility factors, and is independent of the initial attitude except indirectly as it is reflected in the S functions. Since $C_b > C_a$, it is seen that $\triangle(X_0)$ is positive, implying that a recency effect is to be expected in the absence of any alteration in susceptibility to persuasive influence induced by the communication presented first.

Experiments of the type presented in this volume, however, are concerned with the effects of various types of experimental conditions and instructions on changes in susceptibility. For such studies the communicators, the communications, and the audience remain constant, and an attempt is made to change the S values in such a way as to produce primacy or recency effects, or to eliminate both. Therefore, it is desirable to determine what happens to the order effect when the S values are changed by the first communication.

Referring back to equation 10, suppose that the effect of the communication presented first is to *increase* susceptibility. This means that $S_{ba} > S_a$, and $S_{ab} > S_b$. Hence $S_{ba}S_b > S_aS_b$, and $-(S_b - S_{ab}) > 0$. The bracketed coefficient of $(C_b - X_0)$ is therefore positive, and larger than S_aS_b, which would be the coefficient in the base-line case. In the same way, the bracketed coefficient of $(C_a - X_0)$ is positive, and larger than S_aS_b, which would be the coefficient in the base-line case. Since both $(C_b - X_0)$ and $-(C_a - X_0)$ are greater than zero, $\triangle(X_0)$ is positive, and larger than for the base-line case. Hence, if the communication presented first brings about increased susceptibility, the order effect will increase over the base-line expectation. A parallel analysis for the case in which the effect of the communication presented first is to *decrease* the S values shows that the order effect will also exhibit a decrease. But if the S values decrease only slightly, the order effect will remain positive (= recency effect). Only if the decreases in S are sufficiently large will the order effect become negative, indicating a primacy effect.

This analysis suggests, therefore, that if change in attitude increases with the distance between the communication and the person, we should expect a recency effect in the absence of any changes in susceptibility to influence. If we accept this premise, we need not conclude that recency effects are evidence of increased susceptibility attributable to the initial communication presentation; recency effects may be found even when the initial communication *reduces* susceptibility to further influence.[1]

1. It should be stated that the conclusions of these last three paragraphs do not depend critically on the linearity assumption of equation 1. It can be shown that the same general argumentation holds if $(C - X_0)$ is replaced by any function of $(C - X_0)$, which increases monotonically with the magnitude of $(C - X_0)$, and has the same sign as $(C - X_0)$, at least under the specifications given.

Motivational Effects of Different Sequential Arrangements of Conflicting Arguments: A Theoretical Analysis

IRVING L. JANIS

DURING the past two decades, research on attitude change has begun to concentrate on studying motivational changes elicited by communication stimuli. Taking account of this trend, a number of psychologists have suggested that theoretical constructs pertaining to motivational conflict might be highly productive as a source of explanatory hypotheses about the conditions under which communications produce changes in expectation, preferences, and values. (9, 29) For example, Hovland, Janis, and Kelley (18, pp. 283–4) assert that in order to understand the outcome of attempts at changing opinion via communications, various kinds of conflict situations should be explored:

> There already exists a considerable body of behavioral data and psychological theory about the major types of conflicts (e.g., approach-avoidance, avoidance-avoidance)

and their different consequences. In addition, the general effects of conflicting social influences have been investigated in studies of "cross pressures." The available evidence [concerning the effects of persuasive communications] bears out some of the predictions from theories about conflict behavior: there have been observations of vacillation, apathy, and loss of interest in conflict-laden issues, of attempts to avoid conflictful communications, to attribute them to spurious sources, and to distort their meaning. . . . Detailed studies are needed to determine the conditions under which one or another of the various types of conflict solution is likely to occur.

In the present paper an attempt will be made to extend certain aspects of conflict theory to the problems of changing attitudes via persuasive communications, concentrating especially on implications for the effectiveness of different sequential arrangements of opposing arguments. The first part of the discussion will be devoted to specifying several functional properties of the motivational conflicts generated by those persuasive communications which present pro and con arguments. The theoretical concepts will be applied to certain types of communication situations in which such conflicts are especially likely to be generated.

The assumptions, constructs, and inferences to be presented in this discussion form a general theoretical background for the experimental study of primacy effects reported in Chapter 8. The experiment provides some degree of confirmation for one of the main hypotheses inferred from the present theoretical analysis. A number of related hypotheses, which have not yet been tested, will also be formulated on the basis of the same theoretical considerations.

Definitions and Basic Assumptions

What type of conflict is likely to be aroused by a communicator's attempts to change a person's attitudes and what factors determine how the conflict will be resolved? In order to answer such questions, it is necessary to set aside some of the more complicated features of interpersonal communications and to select a type of communication situation which will allow one to perceive most clearly the main variables that determine the outcome. The present discussion will focus exclusively upon one general type of communication situation, which is of a rather simple structure in that the audience readily comprehends what the communicator is advocating and is motivated to take seriously anything he says. Extreme examples of this type of situation would be: (a) an official government request to non-dissident sectors of the public, asking for voluntary cooperation on matters of national defense; (b) a recognized expert's appraisal of a medical, legal, or financial question directed to people who seek information and guidance; (c) social policy recommendations put forth by an acknowledged group leader to his loyal followers. Such instances, although of tremendous social importance, obviously constitute only a limited class of communication situations in our society. The class is restricted to those in which a prestigeful source transmits an intelligible, persuasive message to recipients whose favorable attitude toward the source predisposes them to be relatively uncritical with respect to accepting the truth value and cogency of the main arguments. This class is referred to as "authoritative communications."

It often happens that an authoritative communication presents from the outset a clear-cut stand on the issue under discussion, bolstered by explicit arguments. This means that although the communication may be characterized as two-sided, it does *not* give a neutral or completely nonpartisan presentation: the pro arguments (i.e. those which support the communicator's conclusions) are more frequently and/or more impressively presented than the con arguments (i.e. those which refute any of the pro arguments or which introduce further considerations which foster rejection of the communicator's conclusion). It is this partisan type of two-sided authoritative communication to which the following theoretical analysis is especially intended to apply.

The general principles of motivation and conflict that will be brought to bear in the theoretical analysis are thought to pertain not only to the relatively simple type of persuasion that characterizes authoritative communications but to most, if not all, other types of persuasion as well. However, if the limiting conditions specified in the preceding paragraphs are not met, one must take account of additional complicating variables that would also be important determinants of the motivational conflicts aroused by the communicator's arguments.

As the basis for a theoretical model, the following three general assumptions are made concerning the relationship between communication stimuli and audience motivations:

1. The first assumption is that strong pressure to take a new position on a controversial issue will tend to generate an *approach-avoidance* conflict. Anticipations of gaining social approval or other rewards will motivate the recipient in the direction of accepting a prestigeful communicator's point of view while other considerations, including some which entered into the recipient's initial attitude, will tend to motivate him in the opposite direction. The relative strengths of

the tendencies to approach and avoid adopting the communicator's conclusion will depend, in part, upon the degree to which the recipient is spontaneously aware of the arguments pro and con.

2. The second assumption is that the strength of the motivation to reject a communication will tend to increase whenever a con argument is presented which the recipient had not spontaneously thought of. The cumulative strength of avoidance motives will depend largely upon the degree to which con arguments (negative incentives) become salient at the time when the person is trying to decide whether or not to accept the communicator's conclusions.

3. The third assumption is parallel to the second. The motivation to accept will tend to increase as the recipient becomes aware of the pro arguments (positive incentives) which support the communicator's conclusion.

The above assumptions are intended to pertain to all those audience members who, at the beginning of the communication, are not fully in agreement with the communicator's conclusion and hence are capable of manifesting some degree of change in the direction of the communicator's position. Included would be persons who initially: (a) oppose the position advocated by the communicator; (b) are uninterested in the issue or undecided; (c) favor compromise between the pro and con positions; or (d) favor the same direction as the communicator but are less extreme than he is. Presumably, for persons in all four categories, a conflict would be generated whenever they realize that an authoritative communicator takes a stand on the issue which is more or less different from their own. As soon as the first pro arguments are presented and the recipients become aware of what the prestigeful communicator is advocating, they will experience the arousal of some degree of motivation to bring their own judgments in line with his. But this approach motivation is in conflict with the motivation to retain the original attitude. The latter, which is referred to as avoidance motivation, might derive from many different sources: e.g. a conscious motivation to avoid anticipated personal loss as a consequence of accepting the communicator's position; a partially conscious desire to conform with primary group norms which may be at variance with the communicator's position; an unconscious need to adhere to one's internalized (super-ego) moral standards which might be violated by adopting the communicator's position.

A Theoretical Model of Three Forms of Conflict Resolution

In line with the above theoretical assumptions, the effectiveness of any persuasive communication can be conceptualized as being dependent upon the balance of the opposing motivational forces. The following types of conflict resolution are suggested as a tentative theoretical model to represent what happens when a persuasive communication is completely rejected, evaded, and completely accepted, respectively.

Type 1 (Complete rejection). At one or another time during the communication exposure, the recipient's motivation to reject becomes markedly stronger than the motivation to accept. When the avoidance tendency greatly predominates over the approach tendency, the recipient experiences little hesitation, doubt, or vacillation. Whatever incipient conflict has been generated by the communication will tend to be terminated by a clear-cut decision to reject the communicator's conclusions; thereafter, he will become inattentive and/or unreceptive to any further pro arguments.

Type 2 (Evasion). Throughout the entire communication situation the motivation to reject is almost as strong as the motivation to accept. When neither the approach nor the avoidance tendency predominates, the recipient will evade a clear-cut decision to accept or reject the communicator's conclusions. He will attempt to minimize the degree of conflict or to escape from the conflict-producing situation—e.g. by deciding to adopt a mixed or neutral position, by deciding to postpone reaching any decision between the conflicting points of view until more information becomes available, or by losing interest in the issue altogether.

Type 3 (Complete acceptance). Although initially the recipient's motivation to reject and to accept may be of almost equal strength, the latter motivation is more or less gradually increased above the level of the motivation to reject by the communicator's arguments and appeals. After the initial brief phase of high conflict, the motivation to reject may sometimes increase but never to the point where it approaches the strength of the motivation to accept. With the approach motivation consistently higher than the avoidance motivation, the recipient may undergo some degree of conflict but nevertheless will continue to be highly attentive and responsive to each argument and appeal as it is presented. Thus he not only learns the essential content of the communication but also develops little doubt or hesitation about the dependability of the positive values or anticipated rewards which are implicitly and explicitly put forth by the communicator as positive incentives for conforming with his judgments.

The outstanding feature of Type 1 is that after a brief period of initial conflict (stimulated by becoming aware of the disparity between his own position and that of a prestigeful communicator), the recipient is able to escape the conflict by ignoring or discounting the communication. In Type 2, the recipient undergoes sustained conflict and thereby develops a strong motivation to arrive at a compromise solution or to postpone his decision. In Type 3 these unsuccessful outcomes are prevented supposedly because of the *consistent differential between the strength of the approach and avoidance motivations.*

Implications of the Model: Predicted Outcomes for Three Different Sequences

How do different sequential arrangements of pro and con arguments affect the outcome of approach-avoidance conflicts? One can derive some specific answers to this question by making use of the theoretical model presented in the preceding section. In order to do so, however, it is necessary to distinguish between those communication situations in which the recipient becomes *spontaneously aware* of the opposing arguments and those in which he *remains unaware* of the opposing arguments until the communicator presents them.

If the recipient is himself likely to begin thinking about opposing arguments as soon as the topic of the communication is mentioned, even a one-sided communication is capable of arousing a strong approach-avoidance conflict. For instance, if a recipient is already well informed about the issue and regards it as a matter of considerable personal importance, he will tend to think about the con arguments—which operate as negative incentives—long before the communicator makes any reference whatsoever to them. Under such conditions, if the communicator includes the con arguments in his communication, it may make little difference whether they are presented before or after the pro arguments. Or, as some psychologists have suggested, in such circumstances it may be most effective for the communicator to present the con arguments explicitly *at the beginning* of his communication, in order to prevent the recipients with well-structured opposing beliefs from rehearsing negative objections to themselves at the crucial time when the communicator is presenting his main positive arguments (cf. 19 pp. 203–4).

However, if the opposing arguments are *not* spontaneously salient, even though the recipient may initially disagree with the communicator's conclusion, a different outcome would be expected. Such instances may be of three types: (1) the recipient is initially *unfamiliar* with the opposing arguments; (2) the recipient, although previously familiar with the pros and cons of the issue, is unlikely to recall the opposing arguments because of *weak associative connections;* or (3) the recipient, despite prior learning of relevant opposing arguments, is *lacking in motivation* to recall the pertinent material. Under any of these conditions, the degree of conflict aroused in the recipient will be highly dependent upon the pro and con arguments presented in the communication.

The distinction between salient versus nonsalient opposing arguments should be regarded, of course, as a matter of degree rather than as a rigid dichotomy. When a communication presents a given position on a publicly discussed controversial issue, the recipients may become spontaneously aware of some opposing arguments but they are likely to remain unaware of others. Not all of the opposing arguments will be familiar to the audience, nor will all the familiar ones have sufficiently strong associative connections with the topic under discussion to become spontaneously salient before the communicator calls attention to them. Moreover, when a source with high prestige is communicating with an audience that is generally inclined to be uncritically receptive rather than disputatious, relatively few recipients will become strongly motivated to recall unmentioned arguments which would refute or counteract what the communicator is saying. Thus the con arguments presented in authoritative communications may often be ones that most members of the audience would not spontaneously have thought of themselves. For such communications a purely one-sided presentation might have a better chance of impressing the audience and might mobilize less conflict with respect to accepting the communicator's conclusions than a two-sided presentation. But even when a communicator surmises that such is the case, he may nevertheless decide to include some opposing arguments for purposes of the type described in Chapter 8, e.g. to reduce subsequent disillusionment among those who accept his recommendation or to inoculate the audience against subsequent counterpropaganda. The fact remains, however, that from the communicator's standpoint the introduction of con arguments is apt to be quite risky, because the audience may be awakened to opposing considerations which would otherwise continue to be ignored. In such circumstances, the success of the communicator's efforts to win people to his position would probably depend upon an arrangement of pro and con arguments which is not the same as that which is most effective when almost all the con arguments are spontaneously salient.

According to the theoretical model, when the recipient is aware of con arguments, his avoidance motivation is maximal and the outcome will be rejection or evasion unless his approach motivation can be raised to an even higher level. In order for a communication to be successful in producing attitude change, the communicator must in one way or another convey positive incentives so powerful as to counteract the incentives that motivate the person to maintain his original attitude. The maximal strength of the avoidance motivation aroused during the communication situation is assumed to be a function of the joint strength of (a) spontaneously salient negative incentives and (b) the negative incentives made salient by those con arguments which the audience would otherwise not know or think about. It is only the latter type of negative incentives that the communicator is free to manipulate.

The chances of complete acceptance (Type 3 outcome) depends partly upon whether the negative incentives are presented before or after the positive incentives. If nonsalient con arguments are presented at the very beginning of a communication, the avoidance motivation will become comparatively strong before the main positive incentives have been presented, and thus there will be a high probability that the remainder of the communication will be critically disputed or ignored (Type 1 outcome). When positive arguments and appeals are presented first, however, the audience's motivation to accept the communicator's conclusions will tend to increase to the point where awareness of the negative incentives can be tolerated without impelling the recipient to question the essential parts of the communicator's message. Furthermore, even when the Type 1 outcome is averted, the communicator still runs the risk that as the opposing incentives are made salient, a Type 2 situation of protracted conflict will be created. This risk would presumably be greatest when a communication uses a balanced, alternating sequence —presenting first a positive, followed by a negative argument, then another positive one followed by another negative one, etc. Such a sequence would maximize the chances that the competing motivations would be of almost equal strength for a considerable period of time, especially if the strongest (unrefuted) positive arguments were kept until the end. By withholding con arguments until the positive arguments have aroused the approach motivation to as high a degree as possible, the communicator would minimize the chances of generating a sustained conflict of the type which entails evasive reactions.

When the pro-first order is used, the predominance of approach over avoidance motivation during the early part of the communication may prevent the prolongation of incipient conflict by precipitating a clear-cut decision to accept the communicator's position. The outcome might then be the reverse of Type 1: Once the recipient reaches a conflict-reducing decision to conform with the communicator's judgments, the subsequent con arguments would tend to be discounted or ignored. This proposition is consistent with the "interference" hypothesis put forth as a descriptive generalization by Janis, Lumsdaine, and Gladstone in an earlier research study (25). According to the interference hypothesis, once a belief or verbalizable attitude is changed as a result of exposure to the content of a persuasive communication, the recipient will tend to be resistant to subsequent communications which foster the opposite point of view. This hypothesis was introduced by the authors in the context of explaining their experimental findings which showed that prior exposure to an "optimistic" communication had the effect of minimizing the pessimistic opinion changes evoked by an unfavorable news event (President Truman's announcement in September 1949 that Russia had succeeded in producing an atomic bomb explosion). Thus the "proactive inhibition" to which the interference hypothesis refers was observed in a situation where the opposing content was presented in a separate communication that occurred several months after the first communication exposure. It seems plausible to assume, however, that the same tendency would arise when opposing contents are presented within a single communication exposure. The following subproposition, therefore, is presented as a special case of the interference hypothesis: During exposure to a persuasive communication, if the person once changes his attitude in response to the pro arguments put forth by the communicator, he will tend to become relatively unreceptive and unresponsive to any subsequent opposing arguments presented later on in the same communication, including those impressive con arguments which otherwise would have been most likely to reinforce his initial attitude.

The following set of interrelated propositions summarizes the main inferences drawn from the theoretical analysis of three types of conflict resolution:

1. The probability that recipients will reject an authoritative communication (Type 1 outcome) is highest when nonsalient con arguments are presented at the beginning, before any pro arguments are presented.

2. The probability that participants will evade the obvious implications of an authoritative communication (Type 2 outcome) is highest when nonsalient con arguments are presented alternately with pro arguments.

3. The probability that recipients will accept an authoritative communication (Type 3 outcome) is highest when pro

arguments are presented at the beginning, before any non-salient con arguments are presented.

As a first step toward assessing the theoretical model, the experiment reported in Chapter 8 tested a primacy hypothesis, which follows directly both from the first and third propositions. The second proposition, however, has not yet been experimentally investigated. A rigorous test of this proposition would require comparing an alternating order of pro and con arguments with the sequential arrangements specified in the first and third propositions, and would thus help to determine whether any observed primacy effect is attributable to one or both propositions.

Some Additional Implications

From the theoretical model of conflict resolution, additional implications can be extracted concerning other variables that enter into the arousal of approach and avoidance motivation, provided, of course, that the variables can be adequately defined in terms of the constructs used in the model. For example, it seems likely that some verifiable propositions can be derived concerning the probability of acceptance as a function of interactions between audience motivations and the selection, as well as the spacing, of opposing arguments.

For any argument which asserts that acceptance or rejection of a given conclusion will lead to the satisfaction of some persistent need, it should be possible to predict whether it will have a relatively strong or weak impact on different recipients by taking account of their motivational predispositions. If a con argument refers to the possibility of losing community prestige as a consequence of conforming with the communicator's recommendation, this negative incentive will have a much more powerful effect (with respect to increasing avoidance motivation) in a man whose need for such prestige is strong than in a man whose need is relatively weak. According to the theoretical model, a *weak* con argument could be freely introduced into an authoritative communication at almost any point with comparatively little risk of evoking rejection or evasion of the communication, provided that at least one strong pro argument has already been made salient. But in order for a *strong* con argument to be tolerated without interfering with acceptance of the main conclusion, it might be necessary for the communicator to give beforehand all his strongest pro arguments, so that approach motivation would be built up to a much higher level. Of course it could happen that a given con argument is so strong as to raise avoidance motivation far above the maximal strength of approach motivation and thus result in rejection, no matter what sequential arrangement of arguments is used.

The essential point is that whenever individual differences in the motivational strength of a given argument can be assessed, the theoretical model permits some additional predictions as to what will happen if that argument is presented in different sequential arrangements. Thus the audience might be sorted into predispositional subgroups such as the following: (a) persons who will remain unaffected by the given con argument whether it is presented at the beginning, in the middle, or at the end of the communication; (b) persons who will be adversely affected unless the given con argument is presented near the end of the communication; and (c) persons who will be adversely affected even if the given con argument is presented near the end of the communication. In the light of available research findings on motivational predispositions in relation to attitude change, it seems likely that such predictive categories could be worked out for many persuasive communications on political and social issues. The relative strength of pro and con arguments for each member of an audience might sometimes be estimated with a fair degree of accuracy merely by taking account of such easily observable factors as educational level, age, religion, and various organizational affiliations which are indices of social class aspirations.

There are, of course, many other variables, in addition to those mentioned in the above discussion, which can play a significant role in determining the outcome of a communicator's efforts to persuade his audience. In principle, the theoretical model of alternative conflict resolutions can take account of any effective content variable by postulating that it affects, at least momentarily, the relative strength of either approach or avoidance motivation. However, for the purpose of making a new series of verifiable deductions about the effects of various interacting variables, it would be important to work out some way of measuring the motivational impact of each one of the variables separately. What is especially needed is a set of empirical indices that will enable an investigator to assess the changes in approach motivation produced by communication stimuli independently from the changes in avoidance motivation. If a feasible and dependable method is developed, it should be possible to extend and apply the conflict model in such a way as to make unequivocal predictions about the way many communication variables will interact with the sequential arrangement of those communication stimuli designated as "pro" and "con" arguments. Thus instead of limiting the application of the model to situations where the prestige of the communicator is initially very high, it may be possible to include situations where the communicator's prestige is at a low or intermediate level and to predict for such conditions the comparative effectiveness of different sequences of pro and con arguments. One might then consider how sequence effects are altered when the level of the communicator's prestige changes during the communication exposure as a consequence of what he says about other topics. Thus the theoretical model might be profitably extended to include numerous variables that have been omitted from the relatively simple formulations presented earlier.

It should be noted that the model of conflict resolution, as developed in this paper, is limited to immediate effects of communication stimuli. It is assumed that when a communication has a lasting effect on attitudes, this is at least partly attributable to the persistence of the conflict resolutions which the recipients arrived at while the communication stimuli were salient. But there are many additional factors, such as subsequent exposure to countercommunications, which may determine whether the long-run effects will be the same as or different from the short-run effects (cf. 18, chapter 8). In order to deal more precisely with the temporal course of attitude change, it may be essential to introduce various assumptions about (a) the shape of the approach and the avoidance gradients at various time points during and following exposure to the communication, and (b) the factors which can alter the shapes of the gradients after a given type of conflict resolution has occurred. If the simple theoretical model turns out to be useful for predicting short-run effects, it will probably be worth while to introduce such assumptions in order to deal with the more complex problems of long-run effects.

Questionnaire Used in Chapter 4, Experiment 3

I want you to write a short paragraph of 25 words giving your impression of Jim, the individual about whom you have just read. In other words, tell me what you think of Jim based on the information you just obtained. What kind of a person do you think he is?

What adjectives best describe him?

Do you like him: Yes   No

Is he likeable: Yes   No

Usually when we have an impression of someone, we have some idea of how he looks and behaves. Please write your impressions of Jim for each in a *word* or *two*.

a. How does he look? color of hair _____ complexion _____ body symmetry _____.

b. How does he walk?

c. How does he talk? tone of voice _____ rate of speech _____ quality of speech _____

d. How does he dress?

e. What does he think of himself?

f. What does he think of: Parents? Teachers? Girls his own age? Boys his own age?

1. Jim received an invitation to a party. Did he accept it?

2. While Jim was walking with Harry they met a group of fellow students. Harry stopped to talk with them. What did Jim do?

3. There were two openings for Jim for summer employment. One was an office job where he would work with only one other person; the other was to be a counselor at camp. Which position did Jim accept?

4. Waiting in line to buy a ticket to the movies, someone pushed his way ahead of Jim. What was Jim's reaction?

5. Everyone knew that Jim's acceptance to medical school was exactly what he had hoped for. Harry suggested to Jim that he throw a party and celebrate. Did he?

6. Would Jim in witnessing a football game make remarks which are clearly audible to those around him?

7. One of Jim's teachers asked the class for an idea to start the discussion. Jim had a good idea. Did he present it to the class?

8. Jim called at the shoe repairman's at the time he was told that his shoes would be ready. When he asked for his shoes the repairman told Jim that he had not yet begun to work on them. What did Jim do?

9. Jim felt that Bill was persistently acting in a dictatorial manner toward him in the weekly school science club's meeting. What did Jim do about it?

10. Jim did not agree with what the lecturer was saying. Did he volunteer his opinion?

11. Jim was waiting for his turn in the barber shop. The barber overlooked him to call on another customer who had just come in. What did Jim do?

Will you select from each of the following the word

or words that in your opinion best fit Jim. Put a line under your selection. Also, please state next to your choice the reason why you chose each word you did.

1. (a) friendly (b) more friendly than unfriendly (c) more unfriendly than friendly (d) unfriendly (e) none of these

2. (a) shy (b) more shy than forward (c) more forward than shy (d) forward (e) none of these

3. (a) social (b) more social than unsocial (c) more unsocial than social (d) unsocial (e) none of these

4. (a) aggressive (b) more aggressive than passive (c) more passive than aggressive (d) passive (e) none of these

Now will you please complete the following sentences:

a) In the store, Jim _____

b) With his fellow students, Jim _____

c) When Jim saw the girl he had met the night before, he _____

REFERENCES

Italic numbers at the end of each reference refer to pages in the present volume.

1. Asch, S. E. Forming impressions of personality. *J. Abnorm. Soc. Psychol.*, 1946, *41*, 258–90. *33, 134*
2. Asch, S. E. *Social psychology*. New York, Prentice-Hall, 1952. *79*
3. Bennett, Edith B. Discussion, decision, commitment, and consensus in "group decision." *Hum. Rel.*, 1955, *8*, 251–73. *31, 143*
4. Brembeck, W. L. and Howell, W. S. *Persuasion: A means of social control.* New York, Prentice-Hall, 1952. *153*
5. Carr, H. The laws of association. *Psychol. Rev.*, 1931, *38*, 212–28. *3*
6. Cohen, A. R., Stotland, E., and Wolfe, D. M. An experimental investigation of need for cognition. *J. Abnorm. Soc. Psychol.*, 1955, *51*, 291–4. *79, 82, 93, 136*
7. Cromwell, H. The relative effect on audience attitude of the first versus the second argumentative speech of a series. *Speech Monogr.*, 1950, *17*, 105–22. *3 f., 13 f.*
8. Deutsch, M. and Gerard, H. B. A study of normative and informational social influences upon individual judgment. *J. Abnorm. Soc. Psychol.*, 1955, *51*, 629–36. *31, 143*
9. Dollard, J. and Miller, N. E. *Personality and psychotherapy*. New York, McGraw-Hill, 1950. *170*
10. Doob, L. W. *Public opinion and propaganda*. New York, H. Holt, 1948. *6*
11. Dunlap, K. *Civilized life*. Baltimore, Williams and Wilkins, 1934. *154*
12. Fisher, S., Rubinstein, I. and Freeman, R. W. Intertrial effects of immediate self-committal in a continuous social influence situation. *J. Abnorm. Soc. Psychol.*, 1956, *52*, 200–7. *31, 143, 160*
13. French, J. R. P., Jr. A formal theory of social power. *Psychol. Rev.*, 1956, *63*, 181–94. *160*.
14. Goldberg, S. Three situational determinants of conformity to social norms. *J. Abnorm. Soc. Psychol.*, 1954, *49*, 325–9. *160*
15. Hobart, Enid M. [Enid H. Campbell] and Hovland, C. I. The effect of "commitment" on opinion change following communication. *Amer. Psychologist*, 1954, *9*, 394 (Abstract). *23*

16. Hovland, C. I. Human learning and retention. In *Handbook of experimental psychology*, ed. S. S. Stevens, New York, Wiley, 1951, pp. 613–89. *3, 55*

17. Hovland, C. I. Effects of the mass media of communication. In *Handbook of social psychology*, ed. G. Lindzey. Boston, Addison-Wesley, 1954, pp. 1062–1103. *143*

18. Hovland, C. I., Janis, I. L., and Kelley, H. H. *Communication and persuasion*. New Haven, Yale University Press, 1953. *v, 2, 13, 20, 55, 79, 84, 144, 170 f., 186*

19. Hovland, C. I., Lumsdaine, A. A. and Sheffield, F. D. *Experiments on mass communication*. Princeton, Princeton University Press, 1949. *v, 93, 107, 115, 140 f., 150, 154, 178*

20. Hovland, C. I. and Pritzker, H. A. Extent of opinion change as a function of amount of change advocated. *J. Abnorm. Soc. Psychol.*, 1957, *54*, 257–61, *160*

21. Hovland, C. I. and Weiss, W. The influence of source credibility on communication effectiveness. *Publ. Opin. Quart.*, 1951, *15*, 635–50. *93, 109, 144 f.*

22. Hull, C. L. *A behavior system*. New Haven, Yale University Press, 1952. *99, 164*

23. Janis, I. L. and Feshbach, S. Effects of fear-arousing communications. *J. Abnorm. Soc. Psychol.*, 1953, *48*, 78–92. *79*

24. Janis, I. L. and Feshbach, S. Personality differences associated with responsiveness to fear-arousing communications. *J. Pers.*, 1954, *23*, 154–66. *79*

25. Janis, I. L., Lumsdaine, A. A. and Gladstone, A. I. Effects of preparatory communications on reactions to a subsequent news event. *Publ. Opin. Quart.*, 1951, *15*, 487–518. *181*

26. Kelman, H. C. and Hovland, C. I. "Reinstatement" of the communicator in delayed measurement of opinion change. *J. Abnorm. Soc. Psychol.*, 1953, *48*, 327–35. *109*

27. Klapper, J. T. *The effects of mass media*. New York, Columbia University Bureau of Applied Social Research, 1949 (mimeographed). *22, 155*

28. Lazarsfeld, P. F. *Radio and the printed page*. New York, Duell, Sloan and Pearce, 1940. *22, 155*

29. Lewin, K. *Field theory in social science*. New York, Harper and Bros., 1951. *164, 170*

30. Luchins, A. S. Mechanization in problem solving: the effect of Einstellung. *Psych. Monogr.*, 1942, *54*, 1–95. *8, 57, 62 ff., 73 ff., 134*

31. Luchins, A. S. Definiteness of impression and primacy-recency in communications (in preparation). *71*

32. Luchins, A. S. and Luchins, Edith H. *Rigidity of behavior*. Eugene, Oregon, University of Oregon Press (In press). *62*

33. Lumsdaine, A. A. and Janis, I. L. Resistance to "counterpropaganda" produced by one-sided and two-sided "propaganda" presentations. *Publ. Opin. Quart.*, 1953, *17*, 311–18. *115 f.*

34. Lund, F. H. The psychology of belief. IV. The law of primacy in persuasion. *J. Abnorm. Soc. Psychol.*, 1925, *20*, 183–91. *3 f., 7, 13 ff., 129 ff., 139, 146, 156, 158*

35. Mandell, W. and Hovland, C. I. Is there a "Law of Primacy" in persuasion? *Amer. Psychologist*, 1952, 7, 538 (Title). *13*

36. Murphy, G. *Personality.* New York, Harper and Bros., 1947. *79*

37. Mussen, P. H. Some personality and social factors related to changes in children's attitudes toward Negroes. *J. Abnorm. Soc. Psychol.*, 1950, *45*, 423–41. *79*

38. Pepitone, A. and Hayden, R. G. Some evidence for conflict resolution in impression formation. *J. Abnorm. Soc. Psychol.*, 1955, *51*, 302–7. *152*

39. Sarnoff, I., and Katz, D. The motivational bases of attitude change. *J. Abnorm. Soc. Psychol.*, 1954, *49*, 115–24. *79*

40. Weiss, W. and Fine, B. J. Opinion change as a function of some intra-personal attributes of the communicatees. *J. Abnorm. Soc. Psychol.*, 1955, *51*, 246–53. *79*

41. Weiss, W. and Fine, B. J. The effect of induced aggressiveness on opinion change. *J. Abnorm. Soc. Psychol.*, 1956, *52*, 109–14. *79*

42. Weld, H. P. and Roff, M. A study in the formation of opinion based upon legal evidence. *Amer. J. Psychol.*, 1938, *51*, 609–28. *21*

43. Zajonc, R. B. Cognitive structure and cognitive tuning. Unpublished doctoral dissertation, Univ. of Michigan, 1954. *85*